Reading and Writing
POETRY
With Teenagers

Fredric Lown
Judith W. Steinbergh

J. WESTON
WALCH
PUBLISHER

Portland, Maine

User's Guide
to
Walch Reproducible Books

As part of our general effort to provide educational materials which are as practical and economical as possible, we have designated this publication a "reproducible book." The designation means that purchase of the book includes purchase of the right to limited reproduction of all pages on which this symbol appears:

Here is the basic Walch policy: We grant to individual purchasers of this book the right to make sufficient copies of reproducible pages for use by all students of a single teacher. This permission is limited to a single teacher, and does not apply to entire schools or school systems, so institutions purchasing the book should pass the permission on to a single teacher. Copying of the book or its parts for resale is prohibited.

Any questions regarding this policy or requests to purchase further reproduction rights should be addressed to:

Permissions Editor
J. Weston Walch, Publisher
321 Valley Street • P. O. Box 658
Portland, Maine 04104-0658

1   2   3   4   5   6   7   8   9   10
ISBN 0-8251-2793-9

*We dedicate this book to our students, who continue to
amaze and inspire us with their depth and creativity.*

What is Poetry?

In her *Poetry Handbook*, Babette Deutsch writes that poetry is "the art which . . .
reveals the realities that the senses record, the feelings salute, the mind perceives,
and the shaping imagination orders."

She also quotes Coleridge as saying that poetry is the work of the imagination,
that power which "reveals itself in the balance or reconciliation of opposite or
discordant qualities: of sameness, with difference; of the general, with the concrete;
the idea, with the image; the individual, with the representative; the sense of novelty
and freshness, with old and familiar objects; **a more than usual state of emotion,
with more than usual order;** judgment ever awake and steady self-possession, with
enthusiasm and feeling profound or vehement; and while it blends and harmonizes
the natural and artificial, still subordinates art to nature; the manner to the matter;
and our admiration of the poet to our sympathy with the poetry."

Contents

Acknowledgments

We are grateful to our many colleagues and fellow poets who have taught poetry with enthusiasm and commitment and have generously shared with us their great love of poetry and teaching. In some cases, poetry exercises were developed in partnership with a particular teacher. Other teachers have sent along poetry written by their students, and some of this writing is available here to inspire your students.

We are especially grateful for support from: Carol Bearse, former director of the Magnet Writing Program at the Kane School in Lawrence, Massachusetts, and Naomi Gordon, Language Arts Coordinator in the Brookline, Massachusetts, public schools. We would also like to acknowledge the following Brookline teachers (current and former) for their input: Eric Arnold, Malcolm Astley, Mary Burchenal, Phyllis Kutt, Jane Larsen, Chris McDonnell, Judy McCarthy, Margaret Metzger, Susan Moran, Angela Neilsen, Barbara Scotto, Anita Splendore, Pat Stanley, Beth Thompson, Geoffrey Tegnell, Rich Young, and Martin Sleeper, principal of the Runkle School, to name just a few. We are also deeply grateful to Maria Marrero, Jody Curran, Bambi Good, Denise Zandman,Alice Fastov, Mazal Jaret, Lilia Levitina, Jane Zolot-Gassko, and Josefina Bosch for their invaluable guidance and contribution to the sections in Chapter 4 and 5 on second-language learners.

Special thanks to Victor Cockburn, musician and songwriter for his help on the songwriting process in Chapter 6—his advice and extensive experience in writing songs with students was invaluable to us; Malcolm Astley, who contributed significantly to the development of the Writing a Sonnet section in Chapter 7; and Elizabeth McKim, for a lifetime of collaboration and camaraderie in poetry and teaching.

Our deepest thanks to Elvia West, who typed many of our drafts; and to our editors at J. Weston Walch—Jane Carter Coe, Elizabeth Isele, Kate O'Halloran, Pam O'Neil, and Kiyo Tabéry.

For incredible patience and support, our thanks goes to Beth, Melanie, Zac, and Emma, and to Robin, David, Shauna and Scott, Mayer and Florence. From you and with you comes our love of poetry.

Much of this work has evolved from grades seven to twelve in the Brookline public schools. We have omitted reference to Brookline after Brookline student work. The balance of student examples is drawn primarily from the Kane and Oliver schools in Lawrence, Massachusetts. There is a smattering of student writing from other Massachusetts communities.

All student work is the property of the individual writers. None may be used further without permission from the authors. Not all students chose to have their full name included. Finally, we have made every effort to obtain permission and give full credit for the words and works of other writers that are included in this book. If we have neglected to credit anyone, it was unintentional and we apologize.

To the Teacher

Overview

Reading and Writing Poetry with Teenagers presents an approach to teaching poetry to adolescents in grades seven to twelve. We have included skills related to the reading, listening, discussion, analysis, and writing of poetry. The approach taken in this curriculum, developed by an English teacher and a poet, has been organized as a sequence of self-contained chapters. You, as an individual teacher, can teach all or selected chapters of the book to your class.

We envision a curriculum that integrates the reading, discussion, and analysis of poetry with the writing and crafting of student poems. Poetic technique is explored through broad thematic groupings. Each theme chapter contains poems for discussion and analysis, a bibliography of related poems and books, one or more writing exercises that convey techniques related to the discussion poems, and examples of student writings that evolved from the writing exercises and discussion poems. The unit progresses from the most concrete and accessible themes through more personal and complex ones to the most abstract and intellectual themes. The discussion questions within each chapter also develop from concrete identification to abstract analysis. The sequence of writing exercises within each chapter gives students a growing repertoire of writing techniques to craft their own poems. Student poetry examples, following each writing exercise, exemplify the application of specific writing techniques to theme content. Chapters can be used individually or in a different sequence to adapt to specific needs of your class.

We wrote this curriculum with a firm belief in the value of reading aloud and listening to poetry at all grades and levels of academic achievement. Poetry is written to be read, but more often than not, it is written to be heard. Poetry is the music of our language and can be appreciated more fully when it is both heard and read. Therefore, we have included in the first two chapters a Reading Aloud section that offers poems and suggestions for experimenting with a variety of voices. We also expect that every poem used from the Poems for Discussion and the Writing Exercises sections will be read aloud. In our own classrooms over the course of our poetry studies, we have read aloud hundreds of poems, taken from this selection and from poems written in response to classroom exercises and personal experiences.

> Near the completion of an eight-week poetry unit, I spent a few days discussing Emily Dickinson's work with my eighth-graders. The first poem I read to them was "The wind tapped like a tired man." I wrote this first line on the board and, as a class, we proceeded to discover that this one line employs personification, alliteration, onomatopoeia, and simile. At the end of the period, one boy, with a look of awe on his face, commented, "I never would have appreciated this line if I didn't know how to read poetry. Just think of all the people that this line has no meaning for." In writing *Reading and Writing Poetry with Teenagers* we hope to produce a teaching unit that stimulates reading and writing and creates a love for the language of poetry.
>
> — *Fred Lown*

There is a range of challenge in the poems offered in each chapter. Some are clearly more appropriate for seventh- and eighth-graders. Some poems address issues and concerns of older high school students. The maturity and self-awareness of many juniors and seniors in high school allow them to respond with enthusiastic recognition to poems that acknowledge their place in an adult world.

We have tried, in all sections of the book, to include poems considered classics as well as those with a more contemporary voice. The poems represent a diversity of cultures and both genders. We urge you to let your students hear the widest range of voices in the poems you choose. We have included poems in traditional forms, poems considered experimental, and poems that reflect the cultures from which they evolved.

The poems we've chosen offer lessons in technique, craft, and content. It is interesting to examine and compare the subject matter and imagery used by poets from a variety of cultures. In some cultures at particular times in history, poets may tend to draw heavily from nature; in others, from family and heroes; in some, from the supernatural and the spiritual life; and in others, from social and political issues. These observations may help students find their authentic voices.

> As an eighth-grader, Rafael, after reading "I Ask My Mother to Sing" by Li-Young Lee, wrote a lyrical and devoted poem about his mother who was still back in Argentina. Anita, after discussions of Paul Laurence Dunbar's poem "Sympathy" and Maya Angelou's "Caged Bird," was able to integrate her concerns about urban violence and street life with metaphoric language. If I keep up a dialogue with my students, if I persist in looking and asking, I eventually find a poem that, or a specific poet who, appeals to each student.
>
> —*Judy Steinbergh*

Poetic verse is the most concise form of written expression and does not need to be validated for students, merely made accessible. We feel that *Reading and Writing Poetry with Teenagers* will provide a wealth of resources for your exploration of poetry.

Goals

Our goals in assembling this guide and its collection of poems follow:

1. To make poetry accessible to students as a valid, pleasurable, and comfortable medium of communication.

2. To help students develop listening and speaking skills in order to appreciate the music and oral tradition of our language.

3. To support students in their ability to analyze and assimilate poetry through discussion and written interpretation.

4. To expose students to a diversity of poetic voices that should enhance their appreciation of cultural differences and allow them to connect to a wider community.

5. To encourage second-language learners to express themselves in both their mother tongues and in English.

6. To show students how poetry conveys complex human themes found in all other forms of art and literature.

7. To give students the tools to craft their own poems.

8. To establish a community of trust through the sharing of individual writing styles and personal themes.

Ways to Use This Curriculum

THEME CHAPTERS

Reading and Writing Poetry with Teenagers can be used in a multitude of disciplines and at all middle- and secondary-grade levels. The following themes are included:

Chapter 1.   Nature and the Environment
Chapter 2.   Animals
Chapter 3.   Sports
Chapter 4.   Childhood, Adolescence and Growing Up
Chapter 5.   Relationships
Chapter 6.   Social and Global Issues
Chapter 7.   Form and Content: Sonnets, Villanelles, and Sestinas
Chapter 8.   Praise Poems and Odes
This order has a progression of theme and

technique that begins with the most concrete and least threatening source material and moves to the more personal and then abstract source material. Also, the techniques start with basic skills for making poems and progress toward more sophisticated tools for the crafting and revising of poetry.

POETRY SELECTIONS AND ADDITIONAL RESOURCES

The chapters contain the following:

- Poems for reading aloud
- Poems for discussion
- Bibliography of additional poems
- Model poems for writing exercises
- Student examples

These chapters have been organized to provide you with the most flexibility. While they were meant to integrate the reading and writing of poetry, the discussion poems can be used without the writing exercises, the writing exercises can be used alone, and each chapter can be presented as part of a unit in another school discipline. The addition or substitution of your own poems and themes can only enhance the value of this unit.

This unit is meant to be supplemented with a gathering of poetry anthologies and individual volumes of poetry to give students the widest possible exposure to poetic literature.

We encourage you and your students to bring in your own poetry books as your study begins. You might introduce this curriculum with a discussion of early childhood memories of certain poems or books or even settings where your parents read aloud to you. This is an excellent time for you to encourage students to browse in bookstores and in libraries and to attend poetry readings by poets who might be visiting local cities or towns. We have provided an extensive bibliography of anthologies and selected individual volumes.

Volumes of poetry by individual contemporary poets should reflect the diversity of our culture. Because publication was relatively inaccessible to women and writers of color before the 1960's, most of these volumes will have been published in the last few decades. Audio- and videocassettes of many poets reading their own work are available for rental or purchase.

The work of poets from other countries is becoming available to American readers, due to a growing interest in translation. Many students in American schools have a first language other than English and can appreciate poems in other languages, helping their classmates to read and to understand these poems. Poems that must be read in translation have obvious limitations, yet we should be exposed to the themes of poets in other countries so we can see how poetry reflects, yet transcends, culture and geography.

VARIOUS APPROACHES

You may wish to use this unit in a variety of ways. Here are some possibilities:

- If you choose to undertake a six- to eight-week unit, you might present five or six of the theme chapters. For each theme you introduce to the class, you may select several poems from the Poems for Discussion or from the Writing Exercises model poems. You may have time for only one, perhaps two, writing exercises within each theme, or offer students a choice from the writing exercises.

- You may choose to assign a unifying project to accompany a six- to eight-week poetry unit. This final project can be an individual student writing assignment or a group or even whole-class project. Some ideas include:

    (a) A poetry reading of original work by the class, organized by thematic groupings.

    (b) A class anthology of original poems revised, edited, and laid out by class participants.

(c) Poetry theater or choral reading of published poets' work.

(d) Individual collections or essays that use poetry to make a statement about a theme or to illustrate a particular theory or idea.

• You may wish to select two or three themes for an abbreviated unit.

• You may wish to select particular poems or exercises appropriate for second-language learners. (See Choosing the First Language: Notes for Second-Language Learners at the end of Chapter 4, and Finding Voice in a New Language at the end of Chapter 5.)

• In a survey course, you may wish to emphasize only the discussion and analysis of poems. In an English or creative writing course, you may want to concentrate on the writing and crafting of original student work, selecting appropriate poems from throughout the unit.

• You may find it useful to integrate a particular theme chapter with the content of other disciplines. For example:

Chapter 1, "Nature," and Chapter 2, "Animals," might be integrated into science classes as part of observing and recording the natural environment, or into a literature segment that covers naturalist philosophers such as Henry Beston, Henry David Thoreau, Ralph Waldo Emerson, and Annie Dillard. These chapters might also be used in a current events class that explores ecological concerns.

Chapter 3, "Sports," might be discussed in a social studies class dealing with social relationships, the nature of competition, and cultural priorities.

Chapter 4, "Childhood and Adolescence," could be interspersed with young adult literature or personal narratives about childhood and adolescence, or brought into a developmental psychology course.

Chapter 5, "Relationships," might be used in a social studies context about family structure and values, or cultural roots and traditions.

The poems and exercises might be used in a psychology course to illuminate the nature of family and love relationships.

Chapter 6, "Social and Global Issues," could be integrated into courses such as Problems in Democracy, as well as contemporary and world history courses.

Chapter 7 and Chapter 8, "Form and Content" and "Praise Poems and Odes," could be a unit in any language arts or creative writing course.

Creating an Atmosphere of Trust

One of the most difficult hurdles that a poetry class has to overcome in order to be successful is that of trust. During the first week of a poetry unit, it is not uncommon to hear,

"Poetry is boring."

"Do we have to write poems? Yuck!"

"I did poetry in the fourth grade."

"Don't expect me to read my poems to the class!"

"Six weeks of poetry is six weeks too long."

"Are you kidding, we're going to do poetry every day in here? every day?"

"There is no way I'm going to share anything with this class!"

You should not be discouraged by these types of comments. As a matter of fact, these comments make an excellent starting point for explaining the goals of the unit and discussing issues of trust. A lot of the resistance students have to poetry writing (and other creative writing as well) is the lack of validation for their writing. Dealing with adolescents is dealing with fragile egos, shaky self-esteems, repressed hostility, psychic and emotional ambivalence, and raging hormones.

Once your students realize that they won't be forced to share anything they write during the unit, the initial tension rapidly dissipates. One of the methods we developed with our students is having them write either "personal" or "share" on everything they write. We make it clear that a "personal" paper will be "for our eyes only" and that no one, including the principal and their parents, will ever see that paper. We also make it clear that when we get a "share" piece, we (the teachers) will read it anonymously to the class, if the student wishes.

In the poetry units we have undertaken, our students slowly begin to share more and more of their work. This happens as they hear both our reactions and their classmates' reactions to their writing. Our students often break out into spontaneous "Wows" and applause after student poetry has been read aloud. Not only does this stimulate more students to "share" their poetry, it also encourages students to take credit for their work.

It is important to mention here that a lot of student poetry is experiential. Being experiential, it is often personal and even intimate. We believe that, in poetry, a teacher should never discourage any topic a student may choose to write about, nor should there be any censorship of student writing. While we have read and even shared student poetry that has dealt with such issues as divorce, family violence, mental illness, alcoholism and drug abuse, teenage romance, hatred of parents, death and suicide, we recommend that extreme caution and discretion be taken in dealing with student writing on any of these topics outside of the poetry class.

The sharing of student poetry and the ensuing discussions are an integral part of this approach. It builds up an atmosphere of trust within the class and validates students' ideas and their poetry writing.

REVISING POEMS

Poet John Ciardi advises: "Write! Write hot and revise cold . . . Set it down and then change it. You fill wastebaskets. What slips away, provides. It's hard. It's joyously difficult. It's what Robert Frost called 'the pleasure of taking pains.' Writing requires a soul-consuming effort."

The initial draft of the poem is only the first stage. However, not all poems will be worth revising. Students may wish to accumulate a small body of work, three or four poems, and then select one for revision. How much revision should be expected? This depends partially on a student's skill with language, the comfort of the student in the writing of poetry, and the ultimate

audience for the poem. While revisions are an essential step in the act of writing poetry, students who are new to poetry writing must begin to feel at ease with the risk involved and the emotional content of the poems. As we emphasized in the previous section on Creating an Atmosphere of Trust, you, as the teacher, must create an atmosphere where students are willing to write and share their work. Students are ready at very different times to integrate constructive feedback and revision into the writing process.

Kenneth J. Kantor writes "In Evaluating Creative Writing," that "We may want to accept, at least for a while, genuine expression of feeling. Eventually, of course, we must be able to sense that point at which a student feels confident enough about his own writing that he can nondefensively receive constructive criticism and use it to advantage."

It is not unusual for an adult poet to revise a poem a dozen times. Reading the draft aloud is at the center of this work, leading the writer toward the "final finding of the ear," as Wallace Stevens said. Often, the best revisions are made when some time has passed between the writing and the revision of the poem. This is not always possible in a classroom where a unit concludes in a certain number of weeks. However, the distancing that elapsed time provides allows the writer to see more objectively the strengths and weaknesses of the poem and to revise with a less defensive, more critical eye.

SEQUENCE

The following suggested sequence for revision can be used by individual students or by small groups of students. However, it is best to model it with your whole class, discussing one student poem. Allow at least thirty to forty minutes for one poem. For homework, or the next day in class, students should run through these guidelines with reference to a chosen poem of their own. Then each student can bring one poem to a small revision group. Each student should have a chance to get feedback on a poem over the course of several class meetings.

Revision Guide

1. Choose your favorite poem from three or four you have written. In your revision group, read the poem aloud. Does it make sense? Do any confusing areas need to be clarified? Does the poem have an internal logic? This does not mean that it should have the same kind of vertical logic as a research report; it should have, however, a beginning, a building of tension, and a resolution.

   The ending is very important. It should have a power that emerges from both diction and meaning. Perhaps an original anecdote will find its way into a larger context or raise broader questions. Perhaps the meaning of a feeling or a concept will change through the revelations in the poem. In the most successful poems, the reader is given a new way to see an environment or a fresh way to interpret an emotion or event. The reader should take away a feeling or recognition or a new perspective on the subject of the poem.

2. Read through your poem again. Do any individual "tired" words need to be replaced by stronger or more vivid (juicier) words? Are any words repeated too often? Sometimes the repetition of words or phrases adds to the power and momentum of the poem. If this is not the case, can you find synonyms to replace some of the words? In rhymed poems, if predictable rhymes are used, try to substitute fresh, original rhymes and slant rhymes. (See glossary.)

3. Consider your images. Do any similes or metaphors need to be strengthened or revised to complement each other? If too many diverse images appear in one poem, it may weaken the structure. Make sure abstract concepts and language are rooted in the real world through the use of sense images.

4. Does your poem have some rhythm that helps the reader move along? Some forms require a very regular meter; some subjects suggest more irregular, even jagged rhythms. You may have to eliminate or add words or syllables to create a consistent effect. Are there certain word combinations that give the reader a sense of delight? The poem must be read aloud to hear the rhythmic patterns.

5. Look carefully at your line breaks. Sometimes poets write their first drafts in paragraph form, experimenting with line breaks in later drafts. Read your poem out loud. Where do you want the reader to breathe? Where do you want the reader to pause and think about your phrase or image, about the importance of a certain word? (Words such as "stop" or "edge" may suggest a sudden line break.) Where does the placement of words add to the pleasure of their sounds? Draw in slash marks (/) where you want to try breaking your lines. You might wish to divide the poem into stanzas, trying out stanzas of two, three, or four lines each. Each of these arrangements produces a different effect for the reader. Eventually, you might type several versions of the poem, experimenting with line breaks and choosing the one that pleases you most.

6. Check your use of tenses, and try to make the tense consistent throughout the poem. Point of view and audience for the poem should be conscious and clear.

7. Students experimenting with traditional forms will need to revise a poem several times to understand and integrate the form with the content. Ultimately, the form of the poem should seem organic to the subject matter and style of expression.

8. Correct your spelling, grammar, and punctuation. There are few rules to guide the use of punctuation in poetry. Some poets use very little punctuation, substituting line breaks or spaces on the page to indicate where to pause or breathe. E.E. Cummings, who lowercased his name as well as his poems, used punctuation as a kind of musical notation. Other poets use very traditional punctuation, beginning and ending sentences as you would in prose. In more traditional poems, poets often begin each line with a capital, whether or not it is the beginning of a new sentence. Here, again, the writer must try a number of styles and see which one enhances the meaning of the poem.

9. Rewrite the poem in clear handwriting or printing, or revise it on a typewriter or word processor. The word processor has changed revision from being a cumbersome, tiring process to a time of pleasure and experimentation.

This may sound like an overwhelming number of steps. At first, students may wish to focus on two or three of these guidelines. As students become more proficient in the craft of writing poetry, these steps will become assimilated into their process of successive drafts. Meanwhile, the sequence acts as a reference to the aspects of language, form, and elements of discourse involved in creating a successful poem.

EVALUATING STUDENT WORK

We, as teachers, are often at a loss on how to grade a poem, a collection of original poetry, or a writing project. Your comments, while essential, must often be accompanied by a final grade. To see a student write each week, participate in discussion, share his or her work with the class, and then turn in poor-to-mediocre poetry is the most difficult grading situation that an English/poetry teacher encounters. In order to overcome some of the subjective factors in evaluating poems or final poetry writing projects, we suggest you divide your grading into weekly credits and a final project grade

The weekly credits are based on classroom participation. This could encompass discussion.

analysis of unit poems as well as critiques of student writing. You might require your students to maintain a poetry notebook. Once a week, quickly confer with each student and peruse their notebooks for answers to chapter discussion questions, personal poetry, and creative scribbling.

Other credits could be given for weekly student writing assignments. The evaluation of student poetry might be based on the student's application of writing technique developed in each theme-chapter and evidence of effort toward revision. We tell our students that we will never letter-grade a poem because that presumes we have the last word in poetry writing. In reality, it is very difficult to prioritize personal ideas, intimate expression, and poetic style with a letter grade—not to mention the implicit comparison being made between student poems once a grade has been awarded.

The evaluation of final projects is a relatively straightforward affair. The students are told that if they meet the minimum requirements of the project format, they will receive an A or a B. Some factors you might use in determining a final grade are originality, thematic coherence, sophistication of ideas, work put into the final project, and the student's ultimate potential.

Nature and the Environment

Introduction

Nature is universal to the collective human experience. Poets have always found a rich source of images in their surroundings: the earth, the sea, the rivers, the weather, the heavens. In fact, Rainer Maria Rilke said nature was "infested with poetry." Good nature poems try to make use of all five senses, evoke a place by using specific details pertaining to smell, sound, texture, color, light, and taste. Poets often connect images to each other, or an image to a human experience or feeling through the use of simile and metaphor. These techniques help make the message of the feeling in the poem more concrete.

Poet Sherrod Santos says, "Rather than the poet *closing* his eyes and turning inward, the poet must *open* and turn inward." Nature images provide a centered quality to a poem, whether it is celebratory, meditative, or violent. Images from nature seem to be a kind of common reference point for much of humanity. Storms, wildflowers, and constellations are familiar enough to allow a reader to connect easily to these poems.

The poems included for discussion in Chapter 1, "Nature and the Environment," all draw on nature, using vivid sense imagery. Several poems were chosen for the way nature imagery symbolizes human experience and feeling.

Reading Aloud

Poetry comes from an oral tradition as old as language itself. The Reading Aloud sections found here and in the next chapter, "Animals," serve as an introduction to this oral tradition.

The following Reading Aloud poems were selected for the variety of voices that can be used to read them. "Moon Tiger" contains very vivid and visual imagery that appeals to students. It evokes both fantasy and mystery in the young listener. Ask your students to imagine snow falling in Emily Dickinson's poem "Snow" and to let their imaginations drift with the snowdrifts. "The Lake Isle of Innisfree" was nearly sung by William Butler

Yeats. The repeated "I" phrases have a sing-song chantlike quality. The respectful tone implicit in the Native American poem "The Shining Mountain" allows students to hear how poetry harmonizes with nature. "Mending Wall" is rich in conversation and narration in the context of rural New Hampshire Yankee. The voice in each poem presents its own unique cadence, a music and rhythm that emerges from the choice and arrangement of words.

Reading these poems aloud repeatedly will help students to hear internal and slant rhyme, alliteration, and assonance (repeated vowel sounds). Recognizing these techniques enhances the pleasure and appreciation of poetry.

Have your students read these poems many times, experimenting with different effects, imagining they are reading to various audiences, or arranging the poem for more than one reader.

Moon Tiger

The moon tiger.
In the room, here.
It came in, it is
prowling sleekly
under and over
the twin beds.
See its small head,
silver smooth,
hear the pad of its
large feet. Look,
its white stripes
in the light that slid
through the jalousies.
It is sniffing our
clothes, its cold nose
nudges our bodies.
The beds are narrow,
but I'm coming in with you.

—*Denise Levertov*

Snow

It sifts from leaden sieves,
It powders all the wood,
It fills with alabaster wool
The wrinkles of the road.

It makes an even face
Of mountain and of plain, —
Unbroken forehead from the east
Unto the east again.

It reaches to the fence,
It wraps it, rail by rail,
Till it is lost in fleeces;
It flings a crystal veil

On stump and stack and stem, —
The summer's empty room,
Acres of seams where harvests were,
Recordless, but for them.

It ruffles wrists of posts
As ankles of a queen, —
Then stills its artisans like ghosts,
Denying they have been.

— Emily Dickinson

The Shining Mountain

Let us go together
up the shining mountain

let us sit and watch
the sun go down in beauty

Nanibonsak, the Moon
the Night Traveler
will climb into the skyland

The Awatawesu,
those far-off beings overhead,
the small stars will follow

now we hear
the drums of Thunder
now sparks fly from
the pipe of the Lightning

now Great Owl sings
all must sleep
the Awatawesu and their chief
are in flight across the sky

we sit together in beauty
upon the shining mountain.

— Western Abenaki
translated by Joseph Bruchac

The Lake Isle of Innisfree

I will arise and go now, and go to Innisfree,
And a small cabin build there, of clay and wattles made:
Nine bean-rows will I have there, a hive for the honey-bee,
And live alone in the bee-loud glade.

And I shall have some peace there, for peace comes dropping slow
Dropping from the veils of the morning to where the cricket sings;
There midnight's all a glimmer, and noon a purple glow,
And evening full of the linnet's wings.

I will arise and go now, for always night and day
I hear the lake water lapping with low sounds by the shore;
While I stand on the roadway, or on the pavements grey,
I hear it in the deep heart's core.

— William Butler Yeats

Mending Wall

Something there is that doesn't love a wall,
That sends the frozen-ground-swell under it,
And spills the upper boulders in the sun;
And makes gaps even two can pass abreast.
The work of hunters is another thing:
I have come after them and made repair
Where they have left not one stone on a stone,
But they would have the rabbit out of hiding,
To please the yelping dogs. The gaps I mean,
No one has seen them made or heard
    them made,
But at spring mending-time we find them there.
I let my neighbor know beyond the hill;
And on a day we meet to walk the line
And set the wall between us once again.
We keep the wall between us once again.
We keep the wall between us as we go.
To each the boulders that have fallen to each.
And some are loaves and some so nearly balls
We have to use a spell to make them balance:
"Stay where you are until our backs are turned!"
We wear our fingers rough with handling them.
Oh, just another kind of out-door game,
One on a side. It comes to little more:
There where it is we do not need the wall:
He is all pine and I am apple orchard.
My apple trees will never get across
And eat the cones under his pines, I tell him.
He only says, "Good fences make good
    neighbours."
Spring is the mischief in me, and I wonder
If I could put a notion in his head:
"*Why* do they make good neighbours? Isn't it
Where there are cows? But here there are
    no cows.
Before I built a wall I'd ask to know
What I was walling in or walling out,
And to whom I was like to give offence.
Something there is that doesn't love a wall,
That wants it down." I could say "Elves"
    to him,
But it's not elves exactly, and I'd rather

He said it for himself. I see him there
Bringing a stone grasped firmly by the top
In each hand, like an old-stone savage armed.
He moves in darkness as it seems to me,
Not of woods only and the shade of trees.
He will not go behind his father's saying.
And he likes having thought of it so well
He says again, "Good fences make good
    neighbours."

— *Robert Frost*

Poems for Discussion

1. Swift Things Are Beautiful

Swift things are beautiful:
Swallows and deer,
And lightning that falls
Bright-veined and clear,
Rivers and meteors,
Wind in the wheat,
The strong-withered horse,
The runner's sure feet.

And slow things are beautiful:
The closing of day,
The pause of the wave
That curves downward to spray,
The ember that crumbles,
The opening flower,
And the ox that moves on
In the quiet of power.

— *Elizabeth Coatsworth*

2. The Road Not Taken

Two roads diverged in a yellow wood,
And sorry I could not travel both
And be one traveler, long I stood
And looked down one as far as I could
To where it bent in the undergrowth;

Then took the other, as just as fair,
And having perhaps the better claim,
Because it was grassy and wanted wear;
Though as for that, the passing there
Had worn them really about the same,

And both that morning equally lay
In leaves no step had trodden back.
Oh, I kept the first for another day!
Yet knowing how way leads on to way,
I doubted if I should ever come back.

I shall be telling this with a sigh
Somewhere ages and ages hence:
Two roads diverged in a wood, and I—
I took the one less traveled by,
And that has made all the difference.

— *Robert Frost*

3. The wind tapped like a tired man

The wind tapped like a tired man,
And like a host, "Come in,"
I boldly answered; entered then
My residence within

A rapid, footless guest,
To offer whom a chair
Were as impossible as hand
A sofa to the air.

No bone had he to bind him,
His speech was like the push
Of numerous humming-birds at once
From a superior bush.

His countenance a billow,
His fingers, if he pass,
Let go a music, as of tunes
Blown tremulous in glass.

He visited, still flitting;
Then, like a timid man,

Again he tapped—'twas flurriedly—
And I became alone.

— *Emily Dickinson*

4. Mushrooms

Overnight, very
Whitely, discreetly,
Very quietly

Our toes, our noses
Take hold on the loam,
Acquire the air.

Nobody see us,
Stops us, betrays us:
The small grains make room.

Soft fists insist on
Heaving the needles,
The leafy bedding,

Even the paving.
Our hammers, our rams,
Earless and eyeless,

Perfectly voiceless,
Widen the crannies,
Shoulder through holes. We

Diet on water,
On crumbs of shadow,
Bland-mannered, asking

Little or nothing.
So many of us!
So many of us!

We are shelves, we are
Tables, we are meek,
We are edible,

Nudgers and shovers
In spite of ourselves.
Our kind multiplies:

We shall by morning
Inherit the earth.
Our foot's in the door.

— *Sylvia Plath*

5. From Blossoms

From blossoms comes
this brown paper bag of peaches
we bought from the boy
at the bend in the road where we turned toward
signs painted *Peaches*.

From laden boughs, from hands,
from sweet fellowship in the bins,
comes nectar at the roadside, succulent
peaches we devour, dusty skin and all,
comes the familiar dust of summer, dust we eat.

O, to take what we love inside,
to carry within us an orchard, to eat
not only the skin, but the shade,
not only the sugar, but the days, to hold
the fruit in our hands, adore it, then bite into
the round jubilance of peach.

There are days we live
as if death were nowhere
in the background; from joy
to joy to joy, from wing to wing,
from blossom to blossom to
impossible blossom, to sweet impossible
    blossom.

— *Li-Young Lee*

6. Night Gives Old Woman the Word

Dark whispers
behind the echo
of the wind. Mind
is trapped by patterns
in the sound.
Night works a spell—
Moon spills her naked light.
Reflected fire illuminates
the ground. The pull
of night words makes Earth-Woman
give off heat. Soil glistens
dampened by her sweat.
Corn seed feels the planet's turn
unrolls her root,
prepares to send a shoot
above the dirt. Moon
attracting water in the veins

makes corn leaves uncurl
and probe nocturnal air.
The leaves stretch out
to catch the coming dew.

Clan mother, watching,
hears the planets move.
Old, clan mother listens
to the words—all nature
speaks as slowly seasons
turn—marked by the waxing,
waning Moon; messages
become imprinted on old bones.
Earth words in dark
as well as light. Life
moves through the sky. We plant;
we harvest, and, at last,
we feast. Clan mother listens
and is filled with thanks.
Night murmurs and plants
grow in the fields.
Old Woman hears dark
speak the ancient word.

— *Gail Tremblay*

Questions for Discussion and Analysis

1. How has Elizabeth Coatsworth structured her poem "Swift Things Are Beautiful"? Look at the number of lines, the rhyme pattern, and the meter. Does the structure fit the subject matter? how so? Why does Coatsworth title this poem "Swift Things Are Beautiful" when half of the poem is about slow things? What does the tone of the poem tell us about the narrator's feelings? Every image Coatsworth mentions is beautiful. Is there ugliness in nature? Explain. (See Glossary for tone and meter.)

2. In Robert Frost's poem "The Road Not Taken," what is the format and rhyme scheme, and why do you think the poet chose an odd number of lines for each stanza? What options could these two roads represent? Does the title and last line

suggest a tone of acceptance or regret or neither? Explain. Can you think of decisions you have made that you later came to regret? What actual life events could explain "And that has made all the difference"?

3. (*Note:* After rereading the opening line of Emily Dickinson's poem, "The wind tapped like a tired man," stop and ask students what images, symbols, feelings, and meaning are conveyed by this one line.) Show the different ways Dickinson personifies the wind. For a woman who led such a solitary life in the mid-1800's, what expectations might be evoked by the tapping of the wind? How does the wind reflect the inner feelings of the narrator? Compare this Emily Dickinson poem with her poem "Snow" in the Reading Aloud section. How are the narrative voices different? Are there similarities between the wind tapping in Dickinson's poem and the raven who "suddenly there came a tapping" in Edgar Allan Poe's "The Raven"?

4. "Mushrooms," by Sylvia Plath, can be read on a number of levels. On a literal level, how does this poem trace the growth of mushrooms? What characteristics do mushrooms have that allow them to thrive? What is the voice in this poem? In what other ways are mushrooms personified? According to Plath, will "the meek inherit the earth" as the Bible states? Who are the meek, and how are they like mushrooms? What does the "door" in the last line lead to?

5. What sense imagery does Li-Young Lee use in "From Blossoms"? Describe the narrative sequence of events in the first two verses of "From Blossoms." In the third verse, what might the peach represent? How is Li-Young Lee describing human potential in verse three when he says, "O, to take what we love inside, / to carry within us an orchard . . ."? How are peach blossoms a metaphor for life itself? What do you think

the poet means by "the sweet impossible blossom"?

6. Gail Tremblay, a Native American poet, creates a sense of nocturnal magic through personification in her poem "Night Gives Old Woman the Word." List all the ways in which nature is personified in her poem, for example, "Night works a spell . . . ." Who is the "Old Woman" in the poem? What is the Old Woman's relationship to the "clan mother and to "Earth-Woman," or are they different ways of saying the same thing? What is the message the Old Woman is hearing in the night?

Bibliography of Additional Poems

"Mushrooms," Margaret Atwood
"The Peace of Wild Things," Wendell Berry
"March," Elizabeth Coatsworth
"Stopping by Woods on a Snowy Evening," Robert Frost
"I Have Been One Acquainted with the Night," Robert Frost
"Pied Beauty," Gerard Manley Hopkins
"In Fields of Summer" and "Blackberry Eating," Galway Kinnell
"Sunflowers," Mary Oliver
"Summer Sun," Robert Louis Stevenson
"Georgia Dusk," Jean Toomer
"October," Margaret Walker
"Daffodils," William Wordsworth

Writing Exercises

1. SENSE IMAGERY, SIMILE, AND METAPHOR

When we read or hear a successful poem, we can experience with all of our senses the place described in it close to the way the writer experienced it. In addition to sense images, poets will often compare what they are describing to something else. This is called either simile or metaphor (techniques of figurative language). A simile uses "like" or "as" to make the connection. A metaphor connects two ideas using "is" (or other forms of "to be"), suggesting equivalence, or "of" as connecting words, or may imply a comparison without using any connecting words as in Pablo Neruda's "Ode to a Watermelon": star-filled watermelon . . . *It's* the green whale of the summer . . . . Jewel-box *of* water). When a metaphor is sustained throughout a poem, it is called an "extended metaphor."

The more unusual the simile or metaphor, the more interesting it is to the reader. Similes and metaphors help the reader to experience a place in a fresh or original way, sometimes familiar, sometimes strange. In the following lines, poet Galway Kinnell gives lemons and cabbages new dimensions through similes and metaphors. Notice how vivid and lush Kinnell's use of sense imagery is in describing his pushcart market.

When we read or hear a successful poem, we can experience a place described in it.

The Avenue Bearing the Initial of Christ into the New World

(excerpt)

In the pushcart market, on Sunday,
A crate of lemons discharges light like a battery.
Icicle-shaped carrots that through black soil
Wove away lie like flames in the sun.
Onions with their shirts ripped seek sunlight
On green skins. The sun beats
On beets dirty as boulders in cowfields,

On turnips pinched and gibbous
From budging rocks, on embery sweets,
On Idahos, Long Islands, and Maines,
On horseradishes still growing weeds on the
    flat ends,
On cabbages lying about like sea-green brains
The skulls have been shucked from,
On tomatoes, undented plum-tomatoes,
    alligator-skinned
Cucumbers, that float pickled
In the wooden tubs of green skim milk—

— *Galway Kinnell*

Poetry Exercise #1

Write a poem about a place in nature, using sense images and similes. Choose a place in nature that is vivid in your mind. It may be a place you visited long ago, but you need to remember some details about it. It might be a place in the mountains, by the sea, at a nearby park, by the river, or simply up in a tree. Focus on this one place and describe it, using all of your senses and similes, wherever possible. Try to avoid using clichés in your comparison, such as "the sky was as blue as the sea." If you can't remember all of the details, start with what is still clear in your mind and invent the part that is missing. This is common practice among writers.

A variation on this exercise is to use the classical form of the ode. In this form, the writer addresses the subject of the poem, in this case an element of nature, for example, "Oh spring, you came so unexpectedly," or "Star, you are the guard of the sky." In an ode, the writer often uses figurative language to elevate or glorify the subject. The use of personification is implicit in the ode form. (See Glossary.) Pablo Neruda wrote many wonderful odes in Spanish.

Student Examples

Rainy Day

Soiled clouds hang,
A clap of thunder sounds,
The air is still.
There is not a breath
of wind.
A tree stands,
The monarch of a field.
It moves not one leaf.
Then lightning flashes
through the dark sky.
The clouds gather,
and slowly the rain
begins to fall.

— *Philip*

Winter Forest

The snow falls,
gently, quietly down
to blanket the trees
as nature puts them to bed.

Long, gleaming crystal icicles
hang from my window
like fangs dripping clear blood,
one falls to the ground
and shatters like a glass cup
dropped by the busy housewife.

All is quiet outside
except for the snow falling
gently, quietly down
to blanket the trees.
Nature puts them to bed.

— *Lisa*

Snowflake

I once found a snowflake in a field
an utterly exquisite crystal from god
and yet I found it odd
that it was unlike all
in this field
it was without flaw
with lines made out of lace
and nothing out of place
unique by itself
even though very small
about the size of a minute elf
I shall take it to school with me
and it shall be
the nicest flake they ever beheld
it shall be with me not on a shelf
I shall be the one who holds
the precious flake of glass
but alas
when I got to school the flake was no longer
    there
it was just water like any other melted
snowflake

— *Brendan Dickinson, #11*

Oda a la noche

Noche,
viniste sola en el aire
como guitarro volante.
Llena de brisas
Que me acariciaban en la noche.
Tus grandes ojos
Me miraban desde la ventana.
Llegaste con pequeñas lágrimas
Que refrescaron la natureleza.
Noche,
Llegaste oscura y desolada
Como la capa del día.
Siempre alumbrada
Por pequeñas estrellas brillantes.
Las flores bailaban
Con tu pequeña brisa.
Y tu hermosa luna brillante
Me acompañaba en mis sueños.

— *Karla Figueróa*

Ode to the Night

Night,
You came alone in the air
Like a flying guitar
Full of breezes
That caressed me in the night.
The great eyes
watched me from the window.
You came with small tears
That refreshed nature.
Night,
You came dark and desolate
Like the cape of the day.
Always illuminated by small bright stars.

The flowers danced with your small breeze.
And your beautiful, bright moon came
with me in my dream.

— *Karla Figueróa*
translated by Josefina Bosch

Ode to a Blackberry

Blackberry
Oh I love your taste
Your juices fill my mouth with water and flavor,
Your color tempts me
to suck all the juice and dry you out.
You are the fruit of my dreams,
you are my thoughts and my pleasure,
your tremendous taste has no name.

— *Misael Venturo*

Ode to Ants

Oh what mysterious creatures.
They creep around as little Kings and Queens
of shining armor.
They work twenty-four hours to serve
    their kingdom
and excite themselves with a crumb.
They live happy lives as little peasants
on a distant farm
building castles and villages and storerooms
to fill with leftover food.
Everything from crumbs of pizza
to little leaves for shoes.
The little magical workers working every day
to store food for the long winter days.
Winter comes and they go away
along with trees and the other prey.
But as sure as there's day and night,
as soon as the spring sprouts out,
so do the little creatures pour out.

— *Manny*

2. SYMBOLISM IN NATURE

Poets have often chosen symbols from nature to make a visual picture of an abstract idea or emotion. The place or object has a literal meaning and a meaning beyond its physical re-creation. In this way, poets speak on two levels at the same time.

In the poem "The Negro Speaks of Rivers," Langston Hughes uses rivers to symbolize the flow of human civilization from ancient times.

He even expands the river symbols to represent the flow of time before humans inhabited the earth. He identifies so strongly with the river that the river comes to represent his own life force. The poem becomes an extended metaphor for the continuity of his race.

The Negro Speaks of Rivers

(*to W.E.B. Du Bois*)

I've known rivers:
I've known rivers ancient as the world and
    older than the flow of human blood in
    human veins.

My soul has grown deep like the rivers.

I bathed in the Euphrates when dawns
    were young.
I built my hut near the Congo and it lulled me
    to sleep.
I looked upon the Nile and raised the pyramids
    above it.
I heard the singing of the Mississippi when
    Abe Lincoln went down to New Orleans, and
    I've seen its muddy bosom turn all golden in
    the sunset.
I've known rivers:
Ancient, dusky rivers.

My soul has grown deep like the rivers.

— *Langston Hughes*

Here again, in Linda Hogan's "To Light," the "great seas" and the movement of water is a metaphor for the preservation and retelling of cultural history. The analogy of the stories carried in the great sea with the living whose stories break through the chest demonstrates the importance of natural imagery to help explain the continuity and persistence of human existence.

To Light

At the spring
we hear the great seas traveling
underground
giving themselves up
with tongues of water
that sing the earth open.

They have journeyed through the graveyards
of our loved ones
turning in their graves
to carry the stories of life to air.

Even the trees with their rings
have kept track
of the crimes that live within
and against us.

We remember it all.
We remember, though we are just skeletons
whose organs and flesh
hold us in.
We have stories
as old as the great seas
breaking through the chest
flying out of the mouth,
noisy tongues that once were silenced,
all the oceans we contain
coming to light.

— *Linda Hogan*

Mary Oliver uses the striking images of her
Cape Cod environment to speak about the life
cycle in both plant life and human life. The focus
of the poem quickly changes from milkweed to
the inexorable cycles of the generations. Oliver's
astonishing simile of the drying milkweed pods
as aging women changes the reader's percep-
tion of both plants and aging women.

Milkweed

The milkweed now with their many pods
   are standing
like a country of dry women.
The wind lifts their flat leaves and drops them.
This is not kind, but they retain a certain
   crisp glamour;
moreover, it's easy to believe
each one was once young and delicate, also
frightened; also capable
of a certain amount of rough joy.
I wish you would walk with me out into
   the world.
I wish you could see what has to happen, how
each one crackles like a blessing
over its thin children as they rush away.

— *Mary Oliver*

Poetry Exercise #2

Write a symbol poem choosing some
aspect of nature to represent an emotion, a
human trait, or a global issue. Discuss how
natural phenomena, such as a river, valley,
rock, flower, seedpod, shell, mountain, wind,
drought, or tornado, might stand for anger
or joy (emotion), greed or compassion
(human trait), or war and peace (global
issues). Using wind as an example, a morning breeze could represent peace and
harmony, hurricane winds could represent
the combat of war, and tornadoes could
symbolize nuclear explosions.

Students can focus on one or two natural
images, developing figurative language
that allows the similes or metaphors to
work at both a literal and symbolic level.

Student Examples

Untitled

She bubbles with divine
elegance, speaking to anyone who will notice
her presence.

Her voice is wise and
well traveled, like that
of a gazelle
having had many homes.

Branching out at frequent
intervals, to aid others
and help them prosper.
She never dies.

Her quest to reach a
final destination shall
never end. For there
is always somewhere
to flow.
She is the River

— *Shannon Kos*

Nature

Powerful is the sun, who stretches his
hands out to warm people's hearts,

Powerful is the wind, who fills our
minds with songs,

Powerful is the earth, who feeds all
living creatures,

But even more powerful are spiritual gifts:

Love and caring, without beginning or end,

Healing and wholeness, lasting for eternity,
Everlasting hope and faith.

— *Francisco E. Moris*

There Is a War

There is a war going on
Right there on the sidewalk
under my feet.
The small green soldiers
Advance persistently.

Guerrilla warfare
Finding the weak spots
And pushing through
Wherever there is the
Least resistance.

The green blades
Are sharp under my hands
and their pungent odor
Fills the air
I leave them there
To win or lose.

— *Eva*

The Path of Life

Who knows where this road is going,
Who knows what is on the way,
Through the woods and through the forest,
Going forward night and day.
There are lots of paths to follow,
No one knows which way to turn,
There's no telling what you'll find,
There's no telling what you'll learn.
It'll be hard to pass the mountains,
But you know you'll pass them by,
And you know that once you make it,
It'll be peaceful, then you die.

— Olga Gliks

Animals

Introduction

The human connection to animals has always been strong. In Eskimo tribal cultures, members often believed they had a human soul and an animal soul. An Eskimo poem begins:

In the very earliest times / when both people and animals lived on earth a person could become an animal if he wanted to or an animal could become a human being. / Sometimes they were people and sometimes animals / and there was no difference.

Many poets have observed and written about animals in a number of contexts. People tend to have strong emotions, love or hate, toward specific animals, and often a poet will try to influence the reader to share his or her feeling about a certain animal. Other times, a poet will choose an animal to act as a symbol for an abstract idea or feeling. The use of understatement and irony in this case can intensify the central meaning of the poem. Other poets have selected an animal with whom they share a trait, and write in the persona of that animal, using it partially as a mask in order to disclose very personal information without being totally exposed. The discussion poems and exercises address these various uses of animals in the writing of poems.

Reading Aloud

As in Chapter 1, "Nature and the Environment," the poems in this chapter, "Animals," were selected to elicit diverse voices as well as to exemplify a range of moods. "The Delight Song of Tsoai-Talee" is exactly what its title implies: delightful and life affirming. Each line could be read by a different student who would attempt to dramatize "the shadow that follows a child" or "an eagle playing with the wind." In "Spider," one could experiment with the sounds a spider might make if it could speak. Two students might script the poem so there is some dialogue and some choral reading. Notice how

both Edgar Allan Poe and Duane Niatum see the raven as a symbol of knowledge. Poe's "The Raven" is one of the most haunting and dramatic animal poems ever written, famous for its formalized alliterations and rhyming. It is a dark and dreary, even creepy, poem. Each verse might be read by a different individual or a different group of students, with a chorus chiming in to conclude each verse. Give your students time to experiment with possible configurations and presentations.

In William Blake's "The Tyger," the use of question marks gives the poem a serious, interrogative tone. Notice how the questions affect the cadence of the lines. Maxine Kumin's "You Are in Bear Country" has an air of frivolity to it, with her admonitions, Latin terms, and death-by-bear or death-by-bomb choice in the last verse. Kumin has taken a printed pamphlet and selected and transformed some of the actual language to make a "found poem." A student might read it in the role of a park ranger, underplaying the rhymes, then as a poet, accentuating rhyme and cadence. Oral interpretations of "Jabberwocky" should highlight the dramatic story it tells. There might be a narrator and a speaker. Students enjoy making theater of inventive language.

Poems can also be studied and scripted to emphasize particular devices or structures. All of these possibilities are meant to enhance students' delight with poetry, their willingness to listen to it and respond to its rhythms, diction, patterns, and cadence, not just its meaning. In our classrooms over the years we have had students read and reread poetry without moans and groans of boredom. We have found that students of all ages enjoy listening to themselves and others read and interpret aloud the same material. Reading aloud greatly adds to both the appreciation and the understanding of technique and meaning in poetry.

The Delight Song of Tsoai-Talee

I am a feather on the bright sky
I am the blue horse that runs in the plain
I am the fish that rolls, shining, in the water
I am the shadow that follows a child
I am the evening light, the lustre of meadows
I am an eagle playing with the wind
I am a cluster of bright beads
I am the farthest star
I am the cold of the dawn
I am the roaring of the rain
I am the glitter on the crust of the snow
I am the long track of the moon in a lake
I am a flame of four colors
I am a deer standing away in the dusk
I am a field of sumac and the pomme blanche
I am an angle of geese in the winter sky
I am the hunger of a young wolf
I am the whole dream of these things

You see, I am alive, I am alive
I stand in good relation to the earth
I stand in good relation to the gods
I stand in good relation to all that is beautiful
I stand in good relation to the daughter
    of *Tsen-tainte*
You see, I am alive, I am alive

— *N. Scott Momaday*

Spider

Stop, friends, spin with me past
the morning rain, the morning rain.
Touch the yellow, orange, and green threads—
feel the thunder that passed my house!

And if by chance, by accidental dance,
we meet where the meadow's a violet ledge,
don't be frightened by my traces,
they were woven to delight the sun.

There are things about us
too beautiful to lose;
our many-colored song
not even the Raven knows.

— *Duane Niatum*

The Raven

Once upon a midnight dreary, while I pondered, weak and weary,
Over many a quaint and curious volume of forgotten lore—
While I nodded, nearly napping, suddenly there came a tapping,
As of some one gently rapping, rapping at my chamber door.
"'Tis some visitor," I muttered, "tapping at my chamber door:
Only this and nothing more."

Ah, distinctly I remember it was in the bleak December,
And each separate dying ember wrought its ghost upon the floor.
Eagerly I wished the morrow—vainly I had sought to borrow
From my books surcease of sorrow—sorrow for the lost Lenore,
For the rare and radiant maiden whom the angels name Lenore:
Nameless here for evermore.

And the silken sad uncertain rustling of each purple curtain
Thrilled me—filled me with fantastic terrors never felt before;
So that now, to still the beating of my heart, I stood repeating,
"'Tis some visitor entreating entrance at my chamber door,
Some late visitor entreating entrance at my chamber door:
This it is and nothing more."

Presently my soul grew stronger; hesitating then no longer,
"Sir," said I, "or Madam, truly your forgiveness I implore;
But the fact is I was napping, and so gently you came rapping,
And so faintly you came tapping, tapping at my chamber door,
That I scarce was sure I heard you"—here I opened wide the door—
Darkness there and nothing more.

Deep into that darkness peering, long I stood there wondering, fearing,
Doubting, dreaming dreams no mortals ever dared to dream before;
But the silence was unbroken, and the stillness gave no token,
And the only word there spoken was the whispered word, "Lenore!"
This I whispered, and an echo murmured back the word, "Lenore":
Merely this and nothing more.

Back into the chamber turning, all my soul within me burning,
Soon again I heard a tapping something louder than before.
"Surely," said I, "surely that is something at my window lattice;
Let me see, then, what thereat is, and this mystery explore:
Let my heart be still a moment, and this mystery explore:
'Tis the wind and nothing more."

Open here I flung the shutter, when, with many a flirt and flutter,
In there stepped a stately Raven of the saintly days of yore.
Not the least obeisance made he; not a minute stopped or stayed he;
But, with mien of lord or lady, perched above my chamber door,

Perched upon a bust of Pallas just above my chamber door:
Perched, and sat, and nothing more.

Then this ebony bird beguiling my sad fancy smiling
By the grave and stern decorum of the countenance it wore—
"Though thy crest be shorn and shaven, thou," I said, "art sure no craven,
Ghastly grim and ancient Raven wandering from the Nightly shore:
Tell me what thy lordly name is on the night's Plutonian shore!"
Quoth the Raven, "Nevermore."

Much I marvelled this ungainly fowl to hear discourse so plainly,
Though its answer little meaning—little relevancy bore;
For we cannot help agreeing that no living human being
Ever yet was blessed with seeing bird above his chamber door,
Bird or beast upon the sculptured bust above his chamber door,
With such name as "Nevermore."

But the Raven, sitting lonely on that placid bust, spoke only
That one word, as if his soul in that one word he did outpour.
Nothing further then he uttered—not a feather then he fluttered—
Till I scarcely more than muttered—"Other friends have flown before;
On the morrow *he* will leave me as my hopes have flown before."
Then the bird said, "Nevermore."

Startled at the stillness broken by reply so aptly spoken,
"Doubtless," said I, "what it utters is its only stock and store,
Caught from some unhappy master whom unmerciful disaster
Followed fast and followed faster till his songs one burden bore:
Till the dirges of his hope that melancholy burden bore
Of 'Never—nevermore.'"

But the Raven still beguiling all my sad soul into smiling,
Straight I wheeled a cushioned seat in front of bird and bust and door;
Then, upon the velvet sinking, I betook myself to linking
Fancy unto fancy, thinking what this ominous bird of yore,
What this grim, ungainly, ghastly, gaunt, and ominous bird of yore
Meant in croaking "Nevermore."

This I sat engaged in guessing, but no syllable expressing
To the fowl whose fiery eyes now burned into my bosom's core;
This and more I sat divining, with my head at ease reclining
On the cushion's velvet lining that the lamplight gloated o'er,
But whose velvet violet lining with the lamplight gloating o'er
She shall press, ah, nevermore!

Then, methought, the air grew denser, perfumed from an unseen censer
Swung by seraphim whose footfalls tinkled on the tufted floor.
"Wretch," I cried, "thy God hath lent thee—by these angels he hath sent thee

Respite—respite and nepenthe from thy memories of Lenore!
Quaff, oh quaff this kind nepenthe and forget this lost Lenore!"
Quoth the Raven, "Nevermore."

"Prophet!" said I, thing of evil!—prophet still, if bird or devil!
Whether Tempter sent, or whether tempest tossed thee here ashore,
Desolate yet all undaunted, on this desert land enchanted—
On this home by horror haunted tell me truly, I implore:
Is there—*is* there balm in Gilead?—tell me—tell me, I implore!"
Quoth the Raven, "Nevermore."

"Prophet!" said I, "thing of evil—prophet still, if bird or devil!
By that heaven that bends above us—by what God we both adore,
Tell this soul with sorrow laden if, within the distant Aidenn,
It shall clasp a sainted maiden whom the angels name Lenore:
Clasp a rare and radiant maiden whom the angels name Lenore!"
Quoth the Raven, "Nevermore."

"Be that word our sign of parting, bird or fiend!" I shrieked, upstarting:
"Get thee back into the tempest and the Night's Plutonian shore!
Leave no black plume as a token of that lie thy soul hath spoken!
Leave my loneliness unbroken! quit the bust above my door!
Take thy beak from out my heart, and take thy form from off my door!"
Quoth the Raven, "Nevermore."

And the Raven, never flitting, still is sitting, still is sitting
On the pallid bust of Pallas just above my chamber door;
And his eyes have all the seeming of a demon's that is dreaming,
And the lamplight o'er him streaming throws his shadow on the floor:
And my soul from out that shadow that lies floating on the floor
Shall be lifted—nevermore!

— Edgar Allan Poe

The Tyger

Tyger! Tyger! burning bright
In the forests of the night,
What immortal hand or eye
Could frame thy fearful symmetry?

In what distant deeps or skies
Burnt the fire of thine eyes?
On what wings dare he aspire?
What the hand, dare seize the fire?

And what shoulder, and what art,
Could twist the sinews of thy heart?
And when thy heart began to beat,
What dread hand? and what dread feet?

What the hammer? what the chain?
In what furnace was thy brain?
What the anvil? what dread grasp
Dare its deadly terrors clasp?

When the stars threw down their spears,
And water'd heaven with their tears,
Did he smile his work to see?
Did he who made the Lamb make thee?

Tyger! Tyger! burning bright
In the forests of the night,
What immortal hand or eye
Dare frame thy fearful symmetry?

— William Blake

You Are in Bear Country

They've
been here
for thousands of years.
You're
the visitor.
Avoid
encounters. Think ahead.
Keep clear
of berry patches
garbage dumps, carcasses.
On woods walks bring
noisemakers, bells.
Clap hands along the trail
or sing
but in dense bush
or by running water
bear may not hear your clatter.
Whatever else
don't whistle. Whistling
is thought by some to imitate
the sounds bears make when they mate.

You need to know
there are two kinds:
URSUS ARCTUS HORRIBILIS
or grizzly
and URSUS AMERICANUS
the smaller black
said to be
somewhat less likely to attack.
Alas, a small HORRIBILIS
is difficult to distinguish
from a large AMERICANUS.

Although
there is no
guaranteed life-saving way
to deal with an aggressive bear
some ploys
have proved more
successful than others.
Running's a poor choice.
Bear can outrun a racehorse.

Once you're face to face
speak softly. Take
off your pack
and set it down
to distract the grizzly.
Meanwhile back
slowly toward a large
sparsely-branched tree
but remember
black bears are agile climbers
in which case
a tree may not offer escape.

As a last resort you can
play dead. Drop
to the ground face down.
In this case
wearing your pack
may shield your body from attack.
Courage. Lie still. Sometimes
your bear may veer away.
If not
bears have been known
to inflict only minor injuries
upon the prone.

*Is death
by bear to be preferred
to death by bomb?* Under
these extenuating circumstances
your mind may make absurd
leaps. *The answer's yes.*
Come on in. Cherish
your wilderness.

— *Maxine Kumin*

Jabberwocky

'Twas brillig, and the slithy toves
Did gyre and gimble in the wabe;
All mimsy were the borogoves,
And the mome raths outgrabe.

"Beware the Jabberwock, my son!
The jaws that bite, the claws that catch!
Beware the Jubjub bird, and shun
The frumious Bandersnatch!"

He took his vorpal sword in hand:
long time the manxome foe he sought—
So rested he by the Tumtum tree,
And stood awhile in thought.

And, as in uffish thought he stood,
The Jabberwock, with eyes of flame,
Came whiffling through the tulgey wood,
And burbled as it came!

One, two! One, two! And through and through
The vorpal blade went snicker-snack!
He left it dead, and with its head
He went galumphing back.

"And hast thou slain the Jabberwock?
Come to my arms, my beamish boy!
O frabjous day! Callooh! Callay!"
He chortled in his joy.

'Twas brillig, and the slithy toves
Did gyre and gimble in the wabe;
All mimsy were the borogoves,
And the mome raths outgrabe.

— *Lewis Carroll*

Poems for Discussion

1. Raccoons

Night after night
they travel toward dampness,
the stones of the river,
the silky ponds,
and spread a tent
over the banks of sand
shelving to water—all night
they wander through lilies
and weeds, meander
the black rims
of the midsummer low—
then vanish at dawn, climbing
upland through brambles and into
the secret trees.
Oh when the night wind wakes
and the white moon
flies up through the thickets,

I imagine them walking,
silvery, slumberous,
each a sharp set of teeth,
each a gray dreamer, prowling
over the sands, arranging,
night after summer night,
the myths of the morning.

— *Mary Oliver*

2. Equinox: The Goldfinch

it is as if he had swallowed the sun
which slept the winter inside him
until he forgot what it was like
to live in warmth, and golden.
but his body has the knack of timing.
for weeks now golden feathers
have appeared among the grey and khaki brown
now his back is mottled with ice floes
drifting in water that is not blue
but shining purest yellow

he rides upon the cusp of winter
and he is full of sun
it is too much for him to bear
his throat swells with it
and he pushes the sun out
into the air where it turns
immediately to song. The notes

fall back to him, and he tries again,
head back, throwing the sun
into the air, and it returns
to him, and yet again,
and again, there is no end
to this light that is filling him,
it is the sun he has become the sun.
his song shimmers with light
and his body blossoms
into yellow

— *Cheryl Savageau*

3. Beehive

Within this black hive to-night
There swarm a million bees;
Bees passing in and out the moon,
Bees escaping out the moon,
Bees returning through the moon,
Silver bees intently buzzing,
Silver honey dripping from the swarm of bees
Earth is a waxen cell of the world comb,
And I, a drone,
Lying on my back,
Lipping honey,
Getting drunk with silver honey
Wish that I might fly out past the moon
And curl forever in some far-off farmyard
    flower.

— *Jean Toomer*

4. The Fly

Little Fly,
Thy summer's Play
My thoughtless hand
Has brushed away.

Am not I
A fly like thee?
Or art not thou
A Man like me?

For I dance
And I drink and sing.
Till some blind hand
Shall brush my wing.

If thought is life
And strength and breath,
And the want
Of thought is death,

Then am I
A happy Fly
If I live
Or if I die.

—*William Blake*

5. The Fox

Because the snow is deep
Without spot that white falling through
white air

Because she limps a little—bleeds
Where they shot her

Because hunters have guns
And dogs have hangmen's legs

Because I'd like to take her in my arms
And tend her wound

Because she can't afford to die
Killing the young in her belly

I don't know what to say of a soldier's dying
Because there are no proportions in death.

— *Kenneth Patchen*

6. Wild Things

What is it that makes us love wild things?
That after long patience and a kind of thirst,
after speculating on the slap of water,
    whir of wings,
out of the grainy dusk, some wild
    creature bursts

from the forest. Before we focus on its shape,
almost before it can be named,
it twists back, leaps, makes its escape.
Whatever it was, we know it can't be tamed.

Do we want the whole deer quivering
    under our gaze?
The fox frozen as a statue in its track?
No. Only the glaze of eyes,
    the lightning bolt of legs.
the otter's wake. We want the power to attract.

Wildness to be skimmed, sensed, not faced.
We want to love wildness,
    to feel that we've been graced.

— *Judith Steinbergh*

Note: Sonnet Structure

In "Wild Things," Judith Steinbergh's subject is the "nature of wildness" rather than an actual animal. She chose the sonnet form for this poem, staying fairly close to the traditional Shakespearean sonnet of fourteen lines and a rhyme scheme as indicated. Often contemporary poets use end words that are not exact rhymes. This technique is sometimes called slant rhyme or half-rhyme. This also occurs in popular song lyrics. In the traditional sonnet, there is also a turn in the mood following the second stanza. After setting up the situation, the poet stops and asks what do we really want from "wildness"?

Note: Rhythmic Pattern

While a strict sonnet is written in iambic pentameter (an iamb = an unstressed syllable-followed by a stressed syllable and pentameter is five beats to a line, so that one line would scan as -/-/-/-/-/), the rhythmic pattern in this poem is much looser, reflecting how wild creatures cannot be contained by structure or by the human desire to be close to them. (See glossary.)

Questions for Discussion and Analysis

1. How do Mary Oliver's raccoons make night come to life? Trace the pattern of these nocturnal animals by listing the verbs in Oliver's poem. Is there a pattern to the line breaks, the shape of the poem on the page? What are "the myths of the morning"?

2. Equinox happens twice a year—in spring (March 21) and in autumn (September 23). On these two dates, night and day are of equal length across the earth as the sun crosses the equator. Why did Cheryl Savageau choose a goldfinch to represent this occurrence? (Think of both natural and musical harmony.) "Equinox: The Goldfinch" is not only about a bird but is about spring. Find all the imagery that shows the reader the change of season. In the third stanza, "there is no end" prepares the reader for the lack of closure at the end of the poem. Why is there no period after "into yellow"? Try writing two or three more lines. Do you feel your lines are effective? Why or why not?

3. Which words are repeated more than three times in Jean Toomer's "Beehive"? What is the significance and symbolism suggested by these repeated words? What persona is used by Toomer, and how does this voice differentiate itself from the other bees? How are bees and their hive used as symbols for both human activity and human aspirations? Is there a tension here between two conflicting desires?

4. What is William Blake saying about human life when he asks, "Am not I / A fly like thee?" Does this comparison demean human life, exalt insect life, or serve another purpose? What does the "blind hand" refer to? "The Fly" deals with profound philosophical and theological questions on the meaning of existence. How does the verse and rhyme structure lend itself to Blake's interpretation of the life of a fly and human life itself?

5. Like William Blake's "The Fly," Kenneth Patchen's "The Fox" deals with death and mortality. How is the death of the fox different from that of the fly? How does Patchen's imagery create an innocence in the fox? Does this innocence of the victim imply that the hunters are evil? How does the death of a fox and her unborn babies compare to the death of a soldier on a battlefield?

6. In Judith Steinbergh's "Wild Things" sonnet, not all the rhymes are exact. Point out situations where off-rhyme or slant rhyme occur. How are the rhythms and words evocative of various animals? What is meant by wildness in Steinbergh's "Wild Things"? Is this poem about our ambivalence toward taming the wildness in

nature? How would you characterize
a world that is too tame? Would human
spontaneity and impulsive behavior have
a place in a tame world? How does this
natural wildness reflect or evoke human
emotion and experience?

Bibliography of Additional Poems

"The Fish," Elizabeth Bishop
"Turtle," Peter Blue Cloud
"The Horses Graze," Gwendolyn Brooks
"Why Nobody Pets a Lion at the Zoo,"
  John Ciardi
"Bird" and "Healing Animal," Joy Harjo
"For a Dead Kitten," Sara Henderson Hay
"The Bear," Galway Kinnell
"The Snake," D.H. Lawrence
"The Snake," Denise Levertov
"Crows," David McCord
"Angle of Geese," N. Scott Momaday
"Wild Geese," Mary Oliver
"The Starry Snail," Vasco Popa
"The Bat," Theodore Roethke
"Thirteen Ways of Looking at a Blackbird,"
  Wallace Stevens

Writing Exercises

1. SELECTING IMAGES

A poet can influence the reader to feel one way
or another toward an animal simply by the
choice of images and similes. Both of the
following poems are about bats. In the first
one, D.H. Lawrence uses language that
makes us squirm: "Little lumps that fly in air
and have voices indefinite, wildly vindictive:
/Wings like bits of umbrella. / Bats! / Creatures that hang themselves like an old rag to
sleep: / And disgustingly upside down." In
the second poem, Randall Jarrell uses
language that is loving and gentle: "Her high
sharp cries / Like shining needlepoints of
sound / Go out into the night and, echoing
back, / Tell her what they have touched."

Bat

At evening, sitting on this terrace
When the sun from the west, beyond Pisa,
beyond the mountains of Carrara
Departs, and the world is taken by surprise . . .

When the tired flower of Florence
is in gloom beneath the glowing
Brown hills surrounding . . .

When under the arches of the Ponte Vecchio
A green light enters against the stream,
flush from the west
Against the current of obscure Arno . . .

Look up, and you see things flying
Between the day and the night;
swallows with spools of dark thread
sewing the shadows together.

A circle swoop, and a quick parabola
under the bridge arches
Where light pushes through;
A sudden turning upon itself of a thing
in the air.
A dip to the water.

And you think:
"The swallows are flying so late!"

Swallows?

Dark air-life looping
Yet missing the pure loop . . .
A twitch, a twitter, an elastic shudder in flight
And serrated wings against the sky,
Like a glove, a black glove thrown up
at the light,
And falling back.

Never swallows!
Bats!
The swallows are gone.

At a wavering instant
the swallows give way to bats
By the Ponte Vecchio . . .
Changing guard.

Bats, and an uneasy creeping in one's scalp
As the bats swoop overhead!
Flying madly
Pipistrello!
Black piper on an infinitesimal pipe.

Little lumps that fly in air and have voices indef-
inite, wildly vindictive:
Wings like bits of umbrella.
Bats!
Creatures that hang themselves up
like an old rag to sleep;
And disgustingly upside down.
Hanging upside down like rows of disgusting
    old rags
And grinning in their sleep.
Bats!
In China the bat is a symbol of Happiness.
Not for me!

— *D.H. Lawrence*

Bat

A bat is born
Naked and blind and pale.
His mother makes a pocket of her tail
And catches him. He clings to her long fur
By his thumbs and toes and teeth.
And then the mother dances through the night
Doubling and looping, soaring, somersaulting—
Her baby hangs on underneath.
All night, in happiness, she hunts and flies.
Her high sharp cries
Like shining needlepoints of sound
Go out into the night and, echoing back,
Tell her what they have touched.
She hears how far it is, how big it is,
Which way it's going:
She lives by hearing.
The mother eats the moths and gnats she catches
In full flight; in full flight
The mother drinks the water of the pond
She skims across. Her baby hangs on tight.
Her baby drinks the milk she makes him
In moonlight or starlight, in mid-air.
Their single shadow, printed on the moon
Or fluttering across the stars,
Whirls on all night; at daybreak
The tired mother flaps home to her rafter.
The others all are there.
They hang themselves up by their toes,

They wrap themselves in their brown wings.
Bunched upside-down, they sleep in air.
Their sharp ears, their sharp teeth, their quick
    sharp faces
Are dull and slow and mild.
All the bright day, as the mother sleeps,
She folds her wings about her sleeping child.

— *Randall Jarrell*

Poetry Exercise #1

Write a poem about an animal, carefully
selecting images and similes to influence
the reader's feelings. Choose an animal for
which you have some strong feelings. You
might write a poem selecting images and
similes that will influence the reader to feel
as you do about that animal. Or you might
write two short poems about the same
animal, choosing images for each poem that
will convey opposing emotions. Remember
always to use as many senses as possible in
describing the animal.

Student Examples

Eagles

Big majestic
Soaring,
Wings,
feathers as soft as silk,
claws like knives,
soars as fast as a train,
sharp eyes,
spots food,
she sweeps down,
she claws it,
she would eat some,
bring the rest to her young,
Gracefully she swoops down to her nest,
and glides toward it,
they eat,
She wraps them up in her wings
they sleep.
Tomorrow will be a busy day.

— *Johanna*

The Canada Geese

The Canada Geese flew over me
In their classic formation,
A vast aerial "vee"

Their questioning honks
Muted by the beat of their wings and the
    lapping of the waves

Slowly, they descended
Still holding their places
Twenty long, brown and black jets
Coming in for a landing

Lower and lower
They skimmed over the water
They drop the last few inches
Their necks extended, webbed feet
    pointing forward
Their great wings, two feathery air brakes
Then with a sound between the rush of a
    waterfall
And the skipping of a stone
They make contact with the water
You can smell the salty spray from here
Then, forming into family groups
They head home again.

— *Adam Pollack*

2. ANIMALS AS SYMBOLS

Animals have long been powerful myths in ancient civilizations such as Sumer, Egypt, Maya, and Aztec. Animals are important as parables in tribal culture. The stories of jumping mouse and coyote from Nez Percé tribal lore are good examples of how leaders taught values to their tribes. Animals such as the turtle and the crow play a significant role in some tribal creation myths. In *Aesop's Fables*, animals can be interpreted as having human traits. Besides our normal curiosity and identification with animals, many animals have acquired a powerful symbolism or evoke specific connotations. For example, bears seem to embody power, the sea otter, playfulness, and the whale, intelligence. When poets choose an animal as a symbol for an abstract idea, they are speaking about the animal while presenting a more personal human concept.

The following selections are traditional poems from two different North American tribes. Once you've read them, you might wish to refer back to William Blake's "The Tyger" and "The Fly."

Butterfly Song

Butterfly, butterfly, butterfly, butterfly,
Oh, look, see it hovering among the flowers,
It is like a baby trying to walk and not knowing
how to go.
The clouds sprinkle down the rain.

— *Acoma*

Song of the Ghost Dance

The crow
I saw him when he flew down
To the earth
He has renewed our life
He has taken pity on us

— *Cheyenne*

The following poem by Maya Angelou borrows the central metaphor from Paul Laurence Dunbar's poem "Sympathy," which begins, "I know what the caged bird feels, alas." Angelou uses one creature in two different states, "free" and "caged." These two birds stand for or are symbols for two abstract ideas: freedom and oppression. Before reading this poem, you might discuss with your students various historical periods when people have been denied their human rights.

Maya Angelou's poem is a strong example for teaching rhyme, rhythm, repetition, figurative language, and diction. The metaphors "bars of rage" and "grave of dreams" are perfect examples of how concrete objects rooted in the senses are connected to abstract feelings or ideas. You may use this poem to demonstrate choice of diction. Lyrical words such as "leaps," "floats," "dips," and "dares" illuminate the motion and condition of the free bird. Words such as "stalks," "clipped," and "tied" are sharp and painful words that relate to the state of the caged bird.

Caged Bird

A free bird leaps on the back of the wind
and floats downstream
till the current ends
and dips his wing
in the orange sun rays
and dares to claim the sky.

But a bird that stalks
down his narrow cage
can seldom see through
his bars of rage
his wings are clipped and
his feet are tied
so he opens his throat to sing.

The caged bird sings
with a fearful trill
of things unknown
but longed for still
and his tune is heard
on the distant hill
for the caged bird
sings of freedom.

The free bird thinks of another breeze
and the trade winds soft through the sighing trees
and the fat worms waiting on a dawn-bright lawn
and he names the sky his own.

But a caged bird stands on the grave of dreams
his shadow shouts on a nightmare scream
his wings are clipped and his feet are tied
so he opens his throat to sing.

The caged bird sings
with a fearful trill
of things unknown
but longed for still
and his tune is heard
on the distant hill
for the caged bird
sings of freedom.

— *Maya Angelou*

Poetry Exercise #2

Choose an animal to stand for an abstract idea. You might choose one animal and concentrate on *one* idea, such as peace or war, freedom or oppression, hunger, greed, hatred, love. Or you might choose, as Maya Angelou did, one animal in two different conditions to symbolize two opposite ideas such as freedom and oppression, war and peace, wealth and poverty. You may even choose two different animals to symbolize opposite ideas such as the eagle (power) and the mouse (timidity). Discuss with your classmates the various environments where you might encounter whales, tigers, fireflies, parrots, or seals.

Once you have chosen an animal that stands for a more abstract idea, think about specific words that will convey its condition. Brainstorm a list of these words to be used later in the draft of the poem. Are there similes and metaphors that will help the reader make the connection between your animal and your abstract idea? Perhaps you would like to use a refrain. (See glossary.)

Student Examples

A Powerful Competitor

With one powerful flap it soars for miles.
To look into its unblinking eyes is almost impossible to endure.
Each feather streaming with brown and white edges softly painted on.
A powerful predator.
The sharpness and force of its claws.
The shining sun beaming down on its gleaming wings, soaking up the heat.
Its beak powerful and dark like the
    midnight sky.
Those eyes staring at you, through you.
The hawk.
A powerful competitor.

— *Tina Chin*

Bertalan was an immigrant from Hungary, with barely any English, only several years before he wrote this poem in seventh grade, based on "Caged Bird."

The Dove

Flying through the air,
As graceful as a king,
Glides the dove with outstretched wings,
It seems to sing a blessed song
A song of peace and freedom.

White as milk, fine as silk,
The dove lands on a tree,
It seems like it will never stop
the song of liberty.

Unite, thee nations,
Let peace win,
Respect all
as though they're kin.
Let peace triumph,
Let war fall,
Make a wall that stands so tall,
No evil can penetrate,
Let them never find the gate.

Graceful creature is the dove,
Symbolizing peace and love,
Next time you see one above,
Always let your heart be judge.

Pretty to see, soft to touch.
It just means so much for us.

— *Bertalan Moravanszky*

The Homeless Rat

The homeless rat that scatters about
It runs through garbage in and out,
Food is something needed to survive
But for this rat, it is not that way,
For he has no place to stay,
No food, no water, not even a crumb,
Always remember, he's known as a bum.
No family to care for, no one is there,
Nobody stands by his side to share all his pain,
He's lonesome and carefree, he showers with

the occasional rain.
The one thing that's unknown, this rat has
   a brain!
He suffers and survives through cold
   winter nights,
Unlike all others, no heaters in sight.
Every day of the year he puts up a fight.
Is it fair for this poor little rat to not have
   a home?
and not one single person that might let him in
to give him the shelter and care needed to feel
   wanted and safe?
For this tiny creature lives the life of insanity,
The life no person should ever deserve.
A father, a brother, a sister or aunt?
Does this unfortunate rodent
have anyone there to love him
and treat him with what he deserves?
His tiny heart has nothing in there,
But a place for his family is always reserved.

— *Anita*

3. ANIMALS AS PERSONA

Sometimes our interest in animals is due to sharing some behavior or traits with them. Observe how the following two poets use a specific animal to reveal some aspects of themselves.

Metamorphosis

I have turned into a weasel,
with a weasel's green peeled heart,
a black whorled nose like a thumbprint.

My underbelly's long and sleek
and I've great strength. I love
to stretch and lick my furry length.

You left me in the woods all winter;
I wept cold snot-nosed tears. But strange
how quickly winter disappears.

Eyes nosing into everything,
with paddy paws I lounge among the leaves.
I have forgotten how a human grieves.

— *Kathleen Spivack*

Blackbirds

One day we sang,
"The wind is coming along."
And where we sang, it came.

Then we flew that country, green
grass, black fields;
we slid it by miles past our eyes.

By miles it grandly
came below the edge of our wings,
borne up by thousands of songs
from throats of Northland birds.

We tilted and found our
lake, a world with reeds.
Today we sing it all back at the sky.

— *William Stafford*

In "Metamorphosis," Kathleen Spivack speaks about a private loss through the protective persona of a weasel. William Stafford, in "Blackbirds," imbues these birds with the human power to create and share.

Poetry Exercise #3

Consider the animals of our planet. Choose one that attracts you and seems to share some characteristic of behavior or personality. If you are a shy person, you share some characteristics with a deer; if you like to hang out in groups, you might feel drawn to a dolphin; if you are a person who likes to have an overview of things, you might identify with an eagle or hawk; if you are athletic, perhaps a cheetah; and if you are sly, you might take on the persona of the fox.

Now try writing a poem using the persona of the animal you have chosen; in other words, speak in its voice about your life, what you look like, what you fear and love. Try to speak about the actual animals while revealing something significant about yourself.

Student Examples

Uncaged Bird

They open my cage door,
Something inside me says fly.
Something says don't.
But yet I take off and fly aimlessly into walls
    until I come to a sudden halt.
Then the big people come and say words of
    encouragement.
Sometimes they try to get me on their finger
But the result is almost always the same.
I fly again until I crash once more.
And then the big people bring me to my cage.
And they lock it up once I get in.

— *Gabriel Sapolsky*

Zebra

I am not a horse, a donkey, or a cow!
I am a zebra, that's all.
I deserve respect like any other creature.
Why when anybody sees me, they snicker
    and laugh?
They cry out and laugh and call me hateful
things.
They call me freak.
They call me imprisoned,
They call me many other things.
But I don't care. I still hold my head high.
Then one day a child came by.
All she did was stare in silence.
Finally she took a step forward and asked
"Are you white with black stripes
or are you black with white stripes?"

— *Serena Lynn Raymond*

Leopard

There is the spirit of a leopard in me,
I want to be fast and free,
I want to have spots on me,
I want to have whiskers so I can tell when danger is near,
I want to have sharp teeth and claws
so I can fight my enemies,
I will never leave the leopard in me
anywhere but in my heart.

— Leonard Desrochers

The Buck

I, the buck, run swiftly across the shallow water with my doe at my side.
We share the horrible worry of being shot.
Why do humans have to be so cruel; what have we done to them?
Every muscle in my body flexes like a machine working hard to make something.
The cool green water splashes up at my golden brown fur.
There used to be a fresh fragrance; now the stench of cigars and
pipes from the hunters lingers in the air.
"Bang"—a shot goes off.
I know that my muscles will stop flexing; all my love for my doe and fawn will end.
I know this, but I'm not falling or stopping.
I turn my head; they missed me and hit my doe.
All my love for her lies at the pit of my stomach.
I stop running and walk back to her and see a flow of blood from her head.
"Bang"—another shot goes off.
A sharp pain in my gut, I fall on my doe.
Everything darkens.

— Kenneth A. Kozol

Chapter 3

Sports

Introduction

Having students write poems about sports draws on their deep commitment to athletics and competition—a good step before they are asked to confront more personal and family themes. The intensity and energy of various sports offer a writer the particular challenge of capturing a kinetic event within limits of language. The economy of motion in a sport seems to parallel the compression of language in a poem: no wasted movements, no wasted words. Discussion poems in this section are meant to illustrate this economy of words, the careful choice of diction to capture the essence of a specific sport, the use of rhythm and line break to complement/highlight the nature of the sport. Consider how the writer uses tension and release in the poem to reflect conflict and resolution in a game of individual competition.

Poems for Discussion

1. Training (on the Track)

Rainwings
pain-folded into night colors
running streaked into light and dark
cloud shadows chasing
bright fields of pain
shining wet and moving
hair touching softly
whipping into caress
of steady rhythm flowing
into black river of miles
and white lines of minutes
ticking of pain
in left right rhythm
climbing up above where
must stay here
stay here

stay here
no thoughts
sliding down into pain
only high higher climbing

into wind
where I become the wind
blowing through bright fields of pain
— *Grace Butcher*

2. Analysis of Baseball

It's about
the ball,
the bat,
and the mitt.
Ball hits
bat, or it
hits mitt.
Bat doesn't
hit ball, bat
meets it.
Ball bounces
off bat, flies
air, or thuds
ground (dud)
or it
fits mitt.
Bat waits
for ball
to mate.
Ball hates
to take bat's
bait. Ball
flirts, bat's
late, don't
keep the date.
Ball goes in
(thwack) to mitt,
and goes out
(thwack) back
to mitt.

Ball fits
mitt, but
not all
the time.
Sometimes
ball gets hit
(pow) when bat

meets it,
and sails
to a place
where mitt
has to quit
in disgrace.
That's about
the bases
loaded.
About 40,000
fans exploded.

It's about
the ball
the bat,
the mitt,
the bases
and the fans.
It's done
on a diamond
and for fun.
It's about
home, and it's
about run.

— *May Swenson*

3. Jackie Robinson

ran against walls
without breaking.
in night games
was not foul
but, brave as a hit
over the whitestone fences,
entered the conquering dark.

— *Lucille Clifton*

4. To Kate, Skating Better Than Her Date

Wait, Kate! You skate at such a rate
You leave behind your skating mate.
Your splendid speed won't you abate?
He's lagging far behind you, Kate.
He brought you on this skating date
His shy affection thus to state,
But you on skating concentrate
And leave him with a woeful weight
Pressed on his heart. Oh, what a state
A man gets into, how irate
He's bound to be with life and fate
If, when he tries to promulgate
His love, the loved one turns to skate
Far, far ahead to demonstrate
Superior speed and skill. Oh, hate
Is sure to come of love, dear Kate,
If you so treat your skating mate.
Turn again, Kate, or simply wait
Until he comes, then him berate
(Coyly) for catching up so late.
For, Kate, he knows your skating's great,
He's seen your splendid figure eight,
He is not here to contemplate
Your supersonic skating rate—
That is not why he made the date.
He's anxious to expatiate
On how he wants you for his mate.
And don't you want to hear him, Kate?

— *David Daiches*

5. Pasttime

A girl, nine years of wonder
Still on her face,
Stands directly on the bag at third
Running amazed fingers along the wrinkles
of my old leather mitt.
It is the bottom of the ninth,
And everywhere in the world
The bases are loaded.

— *Emilio De Grazia*

6. 400-Meter Freestyle

THE GUN full swing the swimmer catapults and cracks

s
i
x

feet away onto that perfect glass he catches at
  a
n
  d

throws behind him scoop after scoop cunningly moving

t
 h
  e

water back to move him forward. Thrift is his wonderful
 s
e
 c

ret; he has schooled out all extravagance. No muscle

r
 i
  p

ples without compensation wrist cock to heel snap to
 h
i
 s

mobile mouth that siphons in the air that nurtures

h
 i
  m

at half an inch above sea level so to speak.
  T
h
 e

astonishing whites of the soles of his feet rise

a
 n
  d

salute us on the turns. He flips, converts, and is gone
 a
l
l

in one. We watch him for signs. His arms are steady at

t
 h
  e

catch, his cadent feet tick in the stretch, they know
 t
h
 e

lesson well. Lungs know, too; he does not list for

a
 i
  r

he drives along on little sips carefully expended
 b
u
 t

that plum red heart pumps hard cries hurt how soon

i
 t
  s

near one more and makes its final surge. Time: 4:25:9

— Maxine Kumin

7. World Series: Red Sox vs. Mets – 1986

He walks in the door. The game is about to begin.
He will not hear the closing bars of the anthem,
the rising cheer before "home of the brave,"
he will not see the opening plays. He is changing clothes.
Off with the suit, on with the lucky pants, lucky shirt,
lucky sweater, and where are the lucky socks. The socks!
This is a grown man. Phi Beta Kappa from Brown, a man who
reads *Sky and Telescope*, who can describe the most recent
theory of the universe, who has some grasp on a quantum
leap, this man lies down on the rug in front of the tube
and carefully crosses his left leg over his right. He is
drinking the right beer, the one that won the play-offs,
keeping score with the only pencil that will call up a
reverse K from the blank white box and everywhere,
reasonable citizens, families with logical lives,
students who know the Laws of Physics, Nobel Prize
winners, anthropologists, are poking their caps inside
out, switching them backwards, throwing the vibrating
cat out of the only chair that works: Magic. Magic.
How far we've come from the flinging of salt over the
shoulder, from the chanting in the mouth of the cave to
bring the hunter his prey; *one square of pavement*
toward the next crack . . . step on it, break your mother's
back. For if we lose, it will be the fault of
the missing socks. But if we win, we will forget
the incantations and the outfits we wore, we will
remember the brave knees of Buckner and sliding
curves of Hurst, we will think that we deserved it.
We of the bleeding hearts, of the hearts too battered
to bear even the next pitch.

                        — *Judith Steinbergh*

Questions for Discussion and Analysis

1. In Grace Butcher's poem "Training (on the Track)," identify the motion words. How do the verb forms help the motion of the poem? How do the line breaks of the poem enhance her subject? What devices does the poet use to convey the sense of rhythm and repetition involved in running? What physical aspects of running is the poet most concerned with?

2. What are the key baseball words May Swenson uses in "Analysis of Baseball"? The poem describes baseball plays while making wordplays and fooling around with rhyme. Discuss a few of these examples. Does the shape of Swenson's poem reflect any of the physical aspects of baseball?

3. What facts do you know about Jackie Robinson and his place in baseball? What sports metaphor does Lucille Clifton use in "Jackie Robinson" to let us know about his role in breaking down racial barriers? How does she extend the metaphor to further reveal the baseball player's success in a white world?

4. What extreme rhyme scheme does David Daiches use in "To Kate, Skating Better Than Her Date"? What is the effect on the tone of this poem? Which of the previous discussion poems uses a similar technique in rhyme? What is being implied about traditional male-female relationships?

5. In the short poem "Pasttime," by Emilio De Grazia, who is the girl? What object connects the girl to the speaker? What unwritten thoughts does this image of the wrinkled mitt suggest? How would you interpret the last three lines of this poem?

6. The form of Maxine Kumin's poem "400-Meter Freestyle" is integral to the subject. What do her lines reflect about her sport? Where does the poet's diction (word choice) sound like the movements of the racing swimmer (e.g.: "wrist cock to heel snap" "cadent feet tick in the stretch")?

7. "World Series: Red Sox vs. Mets – 1986," by Judith Steinbergh, is more about human behavior and superstition than about the sport of baseball itself. Where does the poet refer to strange behaviors of baseball fans? How is irony used in this poem? What is the attitude of the speaker in the poem? Does it seem to change?

Bibliography of Additional Poems and Books

This Sporting Life, Contemporary American Poems About Sports and Games, Emilie Buchwald and Ruth Roston, eds.

American Sports Poems, R.R. Knuddson and May Swenson, eds.

"To an Athlete Dying Young," A.E. Housman.

Odes of Pindar, translated by Richard Lattimore, University of Chicago Press (Pindar was born in Thebes in 518 B.C. His poetry, written during the fifth century B.C., is mostly tributes to the first Olympian athletes of ancient Greece. Chariot racing, wrestling, sprinting, and boxing were the most popular sports of these early games. All are written about in Pindar's odes.)

In Search of Color Everywhere—A Collection of African-American Poetry, , E. E. Miller, ed.

Writing Exercises

1. ISOLATING THE SENSES

Creating poems about individual or team sports gives the writer a chance to isolate several senses: A poem about basketball might focus on motion and sound; a poem about swimming might include sound and light; a poem about running could concentrate on the feeling of the runner's muscles and the road beneath.

Poetry Exercise #1

Choose a sport you play or follow. Generate two lists of words and phrases: one list of motion words and one list of sounds associated with the sport. Use these words and phrases as a resource for writing a poem that captures the movement, playing sounds, and crowd participation of the sport you have chosen.

Student Example

He Makes Me Move

He makes me move.
When I watch him,
I shake and bounce
and move around,
not able to sit still
as if I'm part of the motion
of him running,
and gliding,
and faking,
and soaring,
and finishing it all off
with a long, swooping leap
to the basket that ends
in a swift flick
of the wrist
and the ball drops
softly down through the net.
And then he lands, turns,

and smiles and winks at
the camera.
I watch his every move,
Praising his
grace.

— *Ronny Weiner*

2. DICTION/WORDPLAY

Reread May Swenson's poem "Analysis of Baseball" and notice her choice and repetition of "ball," "bat," "mitt," "bases," and "fans." Poets choose words that reflect the action of a poem, enhance the meaning of a poem. Maxine Kumin, in "400-Meter Freestyle," uses "ripples," "siphons," "flips," "pumps," and "surge"—all words that convey water motion.

Poetry Exercise #2

Choose a sport you play or follow. Select six to eight words you think are central to the sport. Write a poem that uses these words repeatedly in playful ways, that may even stretch the meanings of the words you selected. In succeeding drafts, try writing the poem in several different shapes to see which one conveys the subject most effectively.

3. IMAGES

Here again, as in poems written from nature, the use of specific images will strengthen the poem. It also helps to focus on a player, a particular play, or a moment of great tension. Consider the senses of texture and smell, taste and sound to help you re-create the emotions that the situation evokes. How might the excitement of the moment resolve itself in the poem? Narrowing the poetic lens will tighten the language of the poem and convey some sense of the athlete's concentration. Robert Francis does this with great skill in the "The Base Stealer." Ask your students to read this dramatically, as if they were poised between first and second base.

The Base Stealer

Poised between going on and back, pulled
Both ways taut like a tightrope-walker,
Fingertips pointing the opposites,
Now bouncing tiptoe like a dropped ball
Or a kid skipping rope, come on, come on,
Running a scattering of steps sidewise,
How he teeters, skitters, tingles, teases,
Taunts them, hovers like an ecstatic bird,
He's only flirting, crowd him, crowd him,
Delicate, delicate, delicate, delicate—now!

— *Robert Francis*

Poetry Exercise #3

Choose a sport you play or watch. Focus on one aspect of a game or event. Carefully choose your images. Imagine you are a video camera technician with only a small amount of tape. What images must you capture to convey the essence of the scene?

Student Examples

The Wonder of Flight

The Celtics and Bulls match up head to head.
Everybody is standing up cheering, anxious
    to see the end result.
One minute to go in the fourth quarter.

Passing, passing, what . . . Jordan steals the ball,
Sprinting down the court, dribbling from
    the ball,
The tracks of smoke disappear into the faces
    of millions.

No one can catch him, everyone stares, while
    trapped in time.

Faced with the determination, the sweat is
    pumping like waterfalls off his face.
Up, up, leaping, climbing stairs while he drives,
In goes the ball, DUNK, SWISHH
The building roars and shakes like an
    earthquake,
Screams and praises, celebration as he scores.

Everybody should know the Wonder of Flight . . .

— *Kara Nicole Dunn*

Notice how the line breaks of the following poem construct a diving board.

Diving

Climbing the ladder like a caterpillar climbing
    a tree.
Fear is gathering up like dust in an attic.
The board wobbles
an old bridge.
I jump up
a frog after a fly.
Pointing my body
like a needle.
The wind rushing
past is a hurricane.
Water glistens below.
Twisting and turning.
Bracing myself.
Splash!
Silent cheering
Alone and at peace
like a dolphin
Fear is all gone
Swimming back
Fear now returns.

— *Matthew Garvey Snover*

Sky Diving

There is never
a feeling of
soaring,
but the thrill
of falling.
Down, down,
down.
You look up,
see the rainbow
that you pulled
down with you.
You look down
see deserts,
ocean and
valleys.
You are not
alone, clouds
are your
neighbors.

— *Elona Prilutsky*

4. BOASTING POEMS

In early tribal cultures, hunters and athletes often chanted boasting poems or songs. These chants were designed to build confidence and ensure success. "The War God's Horse Song," a traditional Navajo chant, uses bragging and exaggeration in simile and metaphor. Its strong rhythm, created by repetition and parallel structure, gives the poem additional power and permits it to be learned easily in the oral tradition.

The War God's Horse Song

I am the Turquoise Woman's son

On top of Belted Mountain beautiful horses
slim like a weasel

My horse has a hoof like striped agate
his fetlock is like fine eagle plume
his legs are like quick lightning

My horse's body is like an eagle-feathered arrow

My horse has a tail like a trailing black cloud

I put flexible goods on my horse's back

The Holy Wind blows through his mane
his mane is made of rainbows

My horse's ears are made of round corn

My horse's eyes are made of stars

My horse's head is made of mixed waters
        (from the holy waters)
        (he never knows thirst)
My horse's teeth are made of white shell

The long rainbow is in his mouth for a bridle

with it I guide him

When my horse neighs
different-colored horses follow

When my horse neighs
different-colored sheep follow

I am wealthy from my horse

Before me peaceful
Behind me peaceful
Under me peaceful
Over me peaceful
Around me peaceful
Peaceful voice when he neighs
I am everlasting and peaceful
I stand for my horse

—*Navajo*
adapted by Dane and Mary Roberts Coolidge

We carry on this oral tradition in contemporary culture with chants and cheers at spectator sports. The technique of boasting or bragging about a projected or wished-for skill has been adapted in some contemporary poetry. This example by Nikki Giovanni shows the child's determination to be great.

a heavy rap

i can run faster than any gazelle
last time i had a race i left him
on the inside corner of the indy 500
i can outswim any ole fish
give a dolphin a half-hour start
and still beat him across the ocean
i mean i'm so bad i gave a falcon
a half-mile lead and beat him to the top
of the mountain
i roared so loud the lion hung his head
in shame and his wife came and asked me to
    please
leave that part of the jungle as her husband's
    feelings
were so hurt by my together thing

i had a jumping contest with a kangaroo and
jumped clear outa australia and passed the
    astronauts
on their way hack down
i can rap so hard Rap Brown hates to be
in the same town with me
and i'm only ten
this year coming

— *Nikki Giovanni*

Poetry Exercise #4

Choose a sport or any skill that you do well or wish you excelled in. Using repetition and parallel structure in the style of "The War God's Horse Song" and bragging in the style of "a heavy rap," write a boasting poem. Make use of exaggerated physical or mental prowess. Don't be afraid to use fantastic imagery; push out the limits of your expression.

Student Example

(See also Student Examples under Praise Poems.)

Bragging

I can jump so high, eagles ask me,
"What's the weather like up there?"

I can run so fast, I have been cordially
invited to the Kentucky Derby,
and I won't have a seat in the stands.

I am so strong
on weekends I fill in for Atlas.

I have such great aim with a gun,
flies from miles around carry
blindfolds and an extra pack of cigarettes.

In this day and age, people like me
come by so infrequently,

I believe the last one was—
Wait let me think, —

No, in fact,
I am the first to be perfect!

— *Stuart Santee*

Chapter 4

Childhood, Adolescence, and Growing Up

Introduction

Many deep sources for writing reside in personal memories of growing up. Memories of childhood and of adolescence, fears and anticipations related to growing up, and emotions surrounding early life changes can provide the seeds for poems. We find ways to hold on to these memories. Many life cycle stages are documented through family albums and personal journals. Some events evolve into family stories which are embellished each time they are retold. Poems also provide a powerful way to record or rediscover an important memory. They help us keep alive people, places, and moments of great joy and celebration. Further, poems can help us articulate and understand personal or family upheavals. Poems might change the way the writer remembers the past.

The Poems for Discussion re-create early childhood images and longings, adolescent uncertainties, and the struggle for individual independence. There are four Writing Exercises to choose from: (1) re-creating a memory from your past through specific sense imagery, possibly in a narrative style, (2) writing song lyrics to express some of the tension and ambivalence of adolescence, (3) writing about a significant change in your life, (4) writing about leaving the country of your birth.

Poems for Discussion

1. Child on Top of a Greenhouse

The wind billowing out the seat of my britches,
My feet crackling splinters of glass and dried putty,
The half-grown chrysanthemums staring up like accusers,
Up through the streaked glass, flashing with sunlight,
A few white clouds all rushing eastward,
A line of elms plunging and tossing like horses,
And everyone, everyone pointing up and shouting!

— *Theodore Roethke*

2. I'll Stay

I like the plates on the ledge
of the dining room wall (to the north)
standing on edge,
standing as if they thought they could stay.

Confident things can stand and stay!

I am confident.
I always thought there was something
to be done about everything.
I'll stay.
I'll not go pouting and shouting out of the city.
I'll stay.

My name will be Up in Lights!
I believe it!
They will know me as Nora-the-Wonderful!
It will happen!
I'll stay.

Mother says "You rise in the morning—
You must be the Sun!
For wherever *you* are there is Light,
and those who are near you are warm,
feel Efficient."

I'll stay.

— *Gwendolyn Brooks*

3. Rough

My parents kept me from children who were rough
Who threw words like stones and who wore torn clothes.
Their thighs showed through rags. They ran in the street
And climbed cliffs and stripped by the country streams.

I feared more than tigers their muscles like iron
Their jerking hands and their knees tight on my arm.
I feared the salt coarse pointing of those boys
Who copied my lisp behind me on the road.

They were lithe, they sprang out behind hedges
Like dogs to bark at my world. They threw mud
While I looked the other way, pretending to smile.
I longed to forgive them, but they never smiled.

— *Stephen Spender*

4. This Morning

(*for the Girls of Eastern High School*)

this morning
this morning
        i met myself
coming in

a bright
jungle girl
shining
quick as a snake
a tall
tree girl a
me girl
        i met myself
this morning
coming in

and all day
i have been
a black bell
ringing
i survive
        survive
survive

— *Lucille Clifton*

5. Variation on a Theme by Rilke

(*The Book of Hours, Book I, Poem I, Stanza I*)

A certain day became a presence to me;
there it was, confronting me—a sky, air, light:
a being. And before it started to descend
from the height of noon, it leaned over
and struck my shoulder as if with
the flat of a sword, granting me
honor and a task. The day's blow
rang out, metallic—or it was I, a bell awakened,
and what I heard was my whole self
saying and singing what it knew: *I can.*

— *Denise Levertov*

6. The Young Ones, Flip Side

In tight pants, tight skirts,
stretched or squeezed,
Youth hurts.
Crammed in, bursting out,
Flesh will sing and hide its doubt.
In nervous hips, hopping glance
Usurping rouge,
Provoking stance.

Put off, or put on,
Youth hurts. And then
It's gone.

— *James Emanuel*

7. Fifteen

South of the Bridge on Seventeenth
I found back of the willows one summer
day a motorcycle with engine running
as it lay on its side, ticking over
slowly in the high grass. I was fifteen.

I admired all that pulsing gleam, the
shiny flanks, the demure headlights
fringed where it lay; I led it gently
to the road and stood with that
companion, ready and friendly. I was fifteen.

We could find the end of a road, meet
the sky out on Seventeenth. I thought about
hills, and patting the handle got back a
confident opinion. On the ridge we indulged
a forward feeling, a tremble. I was fifteen.

Thinking, back farther in the grass I found
the owner, just coming to, where he had flipped
over the rail. He had blood on his hand, was pale—
I helped him walk to his machine. He ran his hand
over it, called me good man, roared away.

I stood there, fifteen.

— *William Stafford*

8. Street Kid

I stand before the window that opens
To a field of sagebrush—
California country northeast of San Francisco.
Holding to the earth and its shield of silence,
The sun burns my thirteen years into the hill.
The white breath of twilight
Whirs with insects crawling down the glass
Between the bars. But it is the meadowlark
Warbling at the end of the fence
That sets me apart from the rest of the boys,
The cool toughs playing ping pong
And cards before lock-up.
When this new home stops calling on memory,
As well as my nickname, Injun Joe,
Given to me by the brothers,
The Blacks, the Chicanos, the others growing
Lean as this solitude, I step
From the window into the darkness,
Reach my soul building a nest against the wall.

— *Duane Niatum*

9. Nikki-Rosa

childhood remembrances are always a drag
if you're Black
you always remember things like living in Woodlawn
with no inside toilet
and if you become famous or something
they never talk about how happy you were to have your mother
all to yourself and
how good the water felt when you got your bath from one of those
big tubs that folk in chicago barbecue in
and somehow when you talk about home
it never gets across how much you
understood their feelings
as the whole family attended meetings about Hollydale
and even though you remember
your biographers never understand
your father's pain as he sells his stock
and another dream goes
and though you're poor it isn't poverty that
concerns you
and though they fought a lot
it isn't your father's drinking that makes any difference
but only that everybody is together and you
and your sister have happy birthdays and very good Christmases
and i really hope no white person ever has cause to write about me
because they never understand Black love is Black wealth and they'll
probably talk about my hard childhood and never understand that
all the while I was quite happy

— *Nikki Giovanni*

10. Remember

(chant)

Remember the sky that you were born under,
know each of the star's stories.
Remember the moon, know who she is. I met her
in a bar once in Iowa City.
Remember the sun's birth at dawn, that is the
strongest point of time. Remember sundown
and the giving away to night.
Remember your birth, how your mother struggled
to give you form and breath. You are evidence of
her life, and her mother's and hers.
Remember your father. He is your life, also.
Remember the earth whose skin you are:
red earth, black earth, yellow earth, white earth
brown earth, we are earth.
Remember the plants, trees, animal life who all have their
tribes, their families, their histories, too. Talk to them,
listen to them. They are alive poems.
Remember the wind. Remember her voice. She knows the
origin of this universe. I heard her singing Kiowa war
dance songs at the corner of Fourth and Central once.
Remember that you are all people and that all people
are you.
Remember that you are this universe and that this
universe is you.
Remember that all is in motion, is growing, is you.
Remember that language comes from this.
Remember the dance that language is, that life is.
Remember.

—*Joy Harjo*

Questions for Discussion and Analysis

1. "Child on Top of a Greenhouse," by Theodore Roethke, evokes sense imagery, particularly sound. List the sounds as heard by the child. How does he hear them (loud, distantly)? What are the similes in this poem that are staring, plunging, and tossing?

2. In "I'll Stay," Gwendolyn Brooks takes on the persona of a girl affirming her confidence and persistence. Why does the speaker identify with plates on the ledge? What metaphor does the Mother use to characterize her daughter and what does this say about their relationship? What is the effect of the repetition "I'll stay?" Look back at the exercise on Boasting in Chapter 3. What might this kind of positive language do for your self-image?

3. Who is the speaker in "Rough," and what separates him from the other children? In what ways does the boy envy these other children? (Use images and feelings to demonstrate this.) Does Stephen Spender set this boy apart from other children because of his lisp, or is this a universal experience of childhood?

4. Which phrases repeat themselves in "This Morning," by Lucille Clifton? How does this repetition fit the character of this poem's speaker? What does the metaphor of the "black bell" tell us about the speaker, as well as the sound of her voice? Compare the attitude and the message of this poem to those of "I'll Stay." In each poem, find language that hints of hardship.

5. In "Variation on a Theme by Rilke," Denise Levertov uses "day" as a metaphor through the technique of personification. Show how the narrator's "day" takes on a life of its own. Why is this metaphor appropriate to the awakening that the narrator experiences? What do you think "honor" and "a task" might refer to? Compare this poem to "This Morning" by Lucille Clifton. What do the bells represent in both poems? Are there other common images and meanings in these two poems? Have you experienced a day that seemed like "the first day of the rest of your life?"

6. How does James Emanuel personify youth in "The Young Ones, Flip Side"? How does the terseness of the language reflect the briefness of youth and the provocative clothes? The meter and rhyme in this poem are fairly regular. How do the line breaks throw off the reader's expectations?

7. In "Fifteen," William Stafford narrates a story from his teenage years. What are the writer's feelings about the motorcycle, his speculations and fantasies? What happens to resolve the poem? How does Stafford's repetition of his age at the time bind the stanzas and imply the young boy's growth?

8. Duane Niatum's poem "Street Kid" is about alienation and about freedom and confinement. What images suggest freedom, and which ones refer to confinement? How does the meadowlark separate the speaker from the rest of the inmates? How might it comfort or save him?

9. There is a danger of remembering childhood with too much sentimentality. "Nikki-Rosa," by Nikki Giovanni, presents a more cynical point of view, suggesting a white biographer might misinterpret the black author's childhood. How does she think a white writer might portray her early life? What values and events were important to her from her childhood? Do you think outsiders might perceive your life in a way that differs from how you experience it?

10. What values does Joy Harjo impart about her Creek Indian culture in her poem "Remember"? What is the web of connections she creates by the end of the poem? What techniques does Harjo use that are reminiscent of early tribal poetry and chant? Does the meaning of the word "Remember" evolve as the poem progresses?

Bibliography of Additional Poems and Books

Poems

"The Front Yard" and "We Real Cool,"
    Gwendolyn Brooks
"On Flunking a Nice Boy Out of School,"
    John Ciardi
"Counting, Recounting," Marilyn Chin
"Fifth Grade—Autobiography," Rita Dove
"We Wear the Mask," Paul Laurence Dunbar
"The Road Not Taken," Robert Frost
"Knoxville, Tennessee," Nikki Giovanni
"Black Jackets," Thom Gunn
"To Be Young, Gifted, and Black," Weldon J.
    Irvine, Jr.
"Girl, Boy, Flower, Bicycle," M.K. Joseph
"White Port and Lemon Juice," Yusef
    Komunyakaa
"To David, About His Education,"
    Howard Nemerov
"Corner," Ralph Pomeroy
"A Story That Could Be True," William Stafford
"Childhood," Margaret Walker
"There Was a Child Went Forth,"
    Walt Whitman
"Boy at the Window," Richard Wilbur
"Chama, N.M.," Terri Mayette Wilkins
"My Heart Leaps Up," William Wordsworth

Books

Games and Puzzles, Barbara Angell
My House, Nikki Giovanni
I Sing the Song of Myself, David Kherdian
Rose, Li-Young Lee
Smart like Me, D. Lourie and M. Pawlak, eds.
A Fire in My Hands, Gary Soto

Writing Exercises

1. RE-CREATING A MEMORY THROUGH IMAGE AND FIGURATIVE LANGUAGE

Think backward through your life as if it were a film rewinding. Stop for a moment at significant events, interchanges, places, relationships. How far back can you remember? What early memories rise up most readily from your mind? Do you ever dream about childhood events? What places and people remain most vivid in your mind? Are there certain smells or textures, sounds or tastes that evoke a specific incident from your childhood? Even in adulthood, eating a tangerine reminds me strongly of my father sitting in our kitchen late at night, peeling the tangerine skin off in a spiral, releasing the strong, sweet smell through the whole kitchen, and drawing me in to sit with him. [Judy Steinbergh]

Perhaps you remember climbing a tree as a child and finding yourself too scared to come down. A bicycle accident may be a vivid memory, or the first time you knew you could swim. The first day of school and the first good friend you made are memories that often remain. You may recall a visit to your grandmother's or a camping trip to the mountains. Baking cookies with a parent or getting a gift of a new pet, cuddling up with a particular stuffed animal or creating a sanctuary for thinking and reading may be other aspects of your childhood you remember. You may remember a game of cards or playing jacks or some neighborhood game you invented with your friends. The following poem by Barbara Angell is just such a memory.

Birds

It is Spring.
People are out on their porches,
and roller skates go cheow, cheow,
cheow on the pavement.

We are running around the big brick barn
that still smells of horses
even though the mansion was torn down
years and years ago, and there's nothing left
but a crater in an empty field
with a wrought iron fence around it.

We are birds.
We are gray and specked
with white on our wings.
And we are practicing our call,
low and fluty, a special call
known only to two of us, mates—
me and Fred Case, the undertaker's son,
who loved all living things.
He grew orchids in this back yard,
raised fantail pigeons in the garage,
hatched butterflies on the screen porch;
everywhere around him, eggs, seeds,
things unfolding.

He was best at being a bird.
He knew the call,
the change from skin to feathers,
how to become winged.

This is how the game would go:
my sister and Fred's little brother
were marauders—jays, mocking birds,
and they would try to find our nest,
so we must build it in a secret place
and hide the eggs.

They will be hunting, calling,
tracking us down.
We crouch in the bushes by the barn,
hold the pebble eggs in our hands,
hear the noisy cries
come closer . . .

. . . we fly,
feel ourselves grow small and light,

transparent-winged, thin-boned.
The sidewalks move below us in a blur.

We can fly forever,
all afternoon, until twilight
comes up from the ground,
when we hear our mother ring the cowbell,
and her "Yoo hoo! Girls!"
will call us home.

— *Barbara Angell*

The sense images in this poem create the setting, the nature of the game, the character of Fred Case, the undertaker's son, and make the fantasy of their play seem believable.

Notice the way the poet speaks in the present tense, as if the event is happening right now. This is a simple device to make the moment real to the reader. In this poem, Barbara Angell moves from reality to fantasy and back to reality by framing the poem in a setting of real objects (skates, barns, horses) and sound ("Yoo hoo! Girls!").

In the following poem, Wing Tek Lum observes these children playing in section one of "Chinatown Games."

Choosing Sides

(*from "Chinatown Games"*)

Little girls
on the sidewalk
chanting in a circle
an even number of them
each offering a hand outstretched
some palms up
some down.
When by chance
an equal number
show up as down
they gather their teams
ready to play
no hint of ability
just the fun of the game.

— *Wing Tek Lum*

A Fire in My Hands is a wonderful collection of poems by Gary Soto, re-creating vivid moments from his adolescence as a Mexican American. If you can acquire this collection, the first poem, "Black Hair," is set at a sandlot baseball game, where the writer longs to play ball like the big boys. (See Chapter 5, Poems for Discussion, for Gary Soto's poem "Oranges.")

When we think of vivid memories of adolescence, they are often associated with tension between generations, and gestures of independence. Often, in speaking about tension and conflict, it helps to use a symbolic or a metaphoric event. Elizabeth McKim's poem "Storm," which follows, uses the anecdote of the "rolling barrels" to represent a rebellion carried out by her whole sixth-grade class. This poem uses a narrative prose-poem style, which builds momentum with words to parallel the barrels rolling down the hill.

Storm

the picnic at roots apple orchard
when I was twelve/vandal stage
the last hurrah before the blood came
and the whole class there
with miss phelon/the meanest strictest
scariest teacher in the school
and the storm begins/and we
have to find shelter/it's thundering
and lightning/so we find this barn where
apples are stored and we swarm
into it like fruitflies/before miss phelon
can stop us/the storm has released
our real anarchic selves, we feel it
and for the first time/we challenge
her authority/we run up the stairs
shouting and laughing/rolling barrels down
we climb out on the roof/I shinny down a
pole/and splat arrive at her feet
and she's yelling/and I'm afraid
and it's exciting and pleasurable

and I run inside again/and she yells for us to
come down
we pay no attention we are up
we keep rolling barrels down/and two boys
run into the woods/and she's sayin' she's
gonna call the police
and then the storm starts to fade
and we round ourselves up/and
shake ourselves out of a trance
and walk silently back to school
but inside/we are shouting
and aroused and happy and free
and when we sit down in our chairs
she says/looking at us so mean and strict
I have decided not to tell the principal
anything about this little incident
and I trust that no one will repeat
to anyone else what happened
this afternoon/and we all know
she's covering her ass/and giving us
a reprieve/and no one snitches
and no one has to stay after
and all my life I bless the class picnic
at roots apple orchard
when the storm came up
and the barrels went down
and the strong scent of freedom
carried us far in its perfect power
and sudden spell.

— *Elizabeth McKim*

In "Shooting Baskets," Christopher Bursk recalls with intensity his private games below his father's window, striving for both the perfection of the shot and for acknowledgment from his father reading in the room above.

Shooting Baskets

The boy pries up the ice from the driveway
till there's blacktop and he's shooting
with one eye on the rim,
one on the window above him, the lamp there.
No, he doesn't really expect his Dad to put
    down his paper,
that tired, shy man, to come out into such cold,
or even to look down, wave.
But the dribble of a basketball
is the sound of a boy who won't give up,
who believes that if you perform the same act
    over and over
something wonderful happens.
In his games he starts hopelessly behind,
45-7, 62-13, 74-18,
and at half time kneels, draws shadow plays
on the little ice left. He's ashamed of the
    whole team,
how can they look anyone in the eyes after this?

And then it's all two-handed set-shots
from behind the trash barrels, sky hooks at
    garden's edge,
a fastbreak started at a snowdrift
and ending with his crashing
against the garage doors, the sag there
a kind of belly from where he's flung himself
many times before. Taking his own pass
he dribbles around ice patches,
one long stride into the air and across
and he's floating again towards the basket
as if he might lift like a curve forever.
Even in his jumpshot he's rising, his hand
    following
the ball's arc, reaching
after what he just let go. Each evening he listens
for that moment the ball drops
perfectly—not rolling around the rim and

rocking out, not even banked
off the backboard, but falling with the pure
    justice

he's waited for, the pleasure
of hearing—no, actually feeling—
from fifteen feet out, from thirty, in his fingertips
the swish, the ball jostling the strings.
It's that kind of sudden rightness,
an acknowledgment,
and he wants it again,
and in the little fragment of light
his father's lamp casts down
he shoots again and again and again.

                        — *Christopher Bursk*

Poetry Exercise #1

Choose one memory that is of interest to you. You do not need to remember every detail about the memory, but a few real details are essential to make the poem convincing. Write a poem that re-creates this memory for the reader by careful attention to sense image. Let simile and metaphor help you convey the emotions that surrounded the event you have chosen. Look back at the styles of the four poems: "Birds" moves between fantasy and reality; "Choosing Sides" is a brief visual description; "Storm" is written in an effusive, insistent prose style; "Shooting Baskets" uses an extended metaphor to show a child's need for parental recognition. Does one of these styles suit your subject better than another?

Student Examples

Dressing Up

Two elegant princesses in a beautiful castle
We are in the midst of a grand ball
Women in red, yellow, pink and purple lacy-
dresses spinning around
Being held by men in handsome suits
A kaleidoscope of people turning, changing to
different patterns
Up a platform, a throne, deep purple
velvet with glistening gold arms
A portly king on the throne surveying the
room, proud
and majestic like the lion of the jungle.
I look around the room, the decorative gold
swirls curve back on themselves in curlicues
Huge chandeliers hang about me, twinkling
calmly in their own light
I begin to dance and spin merging with the
other couples.
My satin dress flares out like the petals of
a blossoming flower
"Come on girls, it's time to clean up those
old junky clothes"
We reluctantly slip out of our ball gowns, leaving
them limp and lifeless on the floor and put on our
jeans and sweatshirts.
Tomorrow we'll return after nursery school.

— *Nancy Elizabeth Lange*

Two Voices

He told me that I was pretty
  My mother told me I smell like some chemical.
He told me that we will run away together
  My mother told me I better clean up my room.
He told me, "You are my ultimate friend."
  My mother told me, "Get off the phone."
Then he suddenly disappeared
  And then my mother, smelling of warm milk
told me that I was beautiful.

— *Zoya Spivakovsky*

Dad

As his eyes widen
A monster emerges
From the depths of his body
I didn't mean to, I say
You did, he replies
Sorry
Is that all you can say
Yea, I reply meekly,
I'm helpless and powerless
No arguments, no wisecracks,
He breathes heavily though his nostrils,
He goes back into his room
Slamming the door,
I breathe relief and brush back
my hair with my hand.

— *David Lange*

Childhood

Childhood,
It is foolish
and playful.

Always running around
In the hearts of little kids
and sometimes hiding in grown ups.

But with age,
it goes away
until the foolishness is gone,
and nothing but seriousness
is left.

Childhood leaving a person
is like the beauty
leaving a rose.

— *Henry Gabriel*

I Remember Milwaukee

It's a time I still remember vividly.
I was the young one.
And I the smallest was the toy.
My cousin would pick me up like a feather and
throw me on the bed.
I would laugh.
My mother would stand watching,
    laughing along.
Up in the air in Milwaukee, my cousin is
    now grown.
His brother and sister have children of
    their own.
He seems older now.
I still remember those times in Milwaukee.
Now he has moved away.

I still remember it in the air before I hit the bed.
I'm too old now and laugh along.
My brother now throws the kids.
Sometimes I remember old Milwaukee.
But really I remember hitting my head on
    the bed.
My brother turned away when I hit hard.
I hit the frame.
My cousin from Milwaukee is now grown.
Now as the child is sailing through the air,
I sometimes look away and think.
I the youngest am now on my own for I make
    my own decisions.
And no longer freely sail through the air.
For the bed's no longer soft and it's not me who
    belongs there.
I still see my cousin but it's not the same.
I watch the child hit the bed and think.
I'm now the age my launcher was then.
I've never been back to Milwaukee.
And my cousin, I'm not sure.
But as I stand watching the child fly through
    the air,
I think of my old cousin and Milwaukee again.

— *Robert Bookston*

Lullaby Lady

As she sprinkles out a soft, beautiful
    tune,
The baby gurgles in the light of the
    moon.
She tells a story while she twirls
    around,
The babe is enchanted by the beautiful
    sound.
This Lullaby Lady so friendly
    and warm
In her soft, mother-like, lullaby
    form.

When the baby grows up
    and moves away.
The Lullaby Lady is stashed on a shelf
    for another day.

She longs to play another
    tune,
For another baby in the light
    of the moon.
To twirl, and play, and dance
    around.
To have a child love her sound.

This Lullaby Lady so friendly and
    warm,
In her soft, mother-like lullaby
    form.

— *Jessica Kuttner*

2. SONG LYRICS

The expression of the teenage experience and of conflict and rebellion has often come through the lyrics of songs. Students in grades seven through twelve are particularly attuned to lyrics and know many of the songs by contemporary groups and soloists, as well as lyrics by poet/singers of the sixties and seventies, such as Bob Dylan, Judy Collins, the Beatles, and the Last Poets. Rap groups in the late eighties and nineties have focused on some of the ills of our society and the individual's struggle to survive them. In the early nineties, Arrested Development guided rap music toward a sense of empowerment for the young to achieve and change society. Ask your students which current songs relate to their lives most directly. Suggest that they bring in the lyrics and spend some class time discussing themes, language, imagery, and metaphor in song lyrics. Look at the structure of the lyrics, and try to trace the music and form to their roots in blues, folk, gospel, chant, country, or other musical genre.

Poetry Exercise #2

Take an issue related to your growing up and increasing independence, or to an area in which you disagree with a prevailing structure or philosophy, and write song lyrics to express your feelings. Once you choose a form (meter and rhyme scheme), try to keep your verses consistent throughout. Simple ballad forms usually use an ABCB (the simplest, since there is only one rhyme per quatrain), AABB, or ABAB. Write a repeating chorus, and decide how often it should be sung. Folk, country, and rap use these familiar rhyme schemes. Blues might repeat the same line two or three times with a different last line (see Glossary). Blues often has a refrain which begins, "I've got the _____ blues." Fill in the blank with something like "early morning," "after-school," "falling-in-love," "homework's-lost" blues. For music, you can experiment with tunes or chords, or you can ask a friend who plays an instrument to try putting your lyrics to music. Tape-record these attempts, and decide if you like any of them enough to play for the class. Otherwise, just present your lyrics.

Student Examples

Young People's Blues

Chorus: We're just young people
                    singing the blues.
          We're just young people,
                    bein' blue ain't news.

You go to bed at night,
And think about the next day,
You try to finish your homework,
But sometimes there ain't no way.

It's hard to concentrate on school,
When you got the Young People's Blues,
But no one wants to hear it,
Bein' blue ain't new news.

Some kids are satisfied
With computers and video machines,
Or a winter house in Florida
A credit card from Filene's

For others it's not material possessions,
It's a satisfaction in life.
For still others not satisfied,
It's a quick slice of a knife.

Everyone has problems,
I know that's not news.
But I do know that we're the only ones . . .
Who have the Young People's Blues.

— *Patrick Doyle*

Parents and the Teenager

Listen mom, I know you care
Your love for me, by far is rare!
You must let go, don't keep me in,
for then my love is what you'll win.

Don't worry dad, I don't smoke pot,
And I'll be in by 10 o'clock,
I clean my room and feed the cat,
Oops! Gotta go, don't have time to chat.

Just leave the key beneath the door.
And I'll be home on time for sure.

—*Tobe Proctor*

Change

Try to change for
the sake of others
Not only for you
but for your many colored brothers.
White and black
are just two colors.
Think of the world
and of the many others.
People have tried to
no one has succeeded
to sort out the problems
that we are feeling.
I think a child can
make a difference,
but we all need
an adult's assistance.

— Tim Collins

Let Me Stand in Peace

(from a longer version)

Yeah I'm somebody or am I not.
This world is crazy,
beatings on the highways
and in the parking lots.

Racism's got people
wrapped around its hand,
From now to then
when the whites got their land.

to an awful story
where no one is friends,
when suddenly smiles and laughter
come to an end.

Smiles into tears,
handshakes into fists
Yeah, I know we all want to make it,
but there's no one to assist.

People wondering,
hurting from all the disbelief,
While colored and uncolored
walk with great grief.

Little kids losing playmates,
because of their different complexion,
But you're colored too, so there's
no need for self-protection.

Everyone's got a different color
on their face,
People aren't judging you,
they're judging your race.

But now it's time to come together
and accept each other holding hands,
Forget about the hate group,
and the Ku Klux Klan.

Remember, I'm just a kid,
know where these words are comin' from,
I've always given acceptance,
now don't you think you ought to give some.

In every way, we're the same,
so show some respect,
Acknowledge that it's
our own feelings we neglect.

Let me stand in peace where people
needn't worry about their race,
Where peace and equality
is seen on every face.

— Ana Piñero

3. Changes

Your students may identify a moment in their past that actually changed their lives or headed them in a new direction. They may have emigrated to a new country or moved to a new town or new school. Perhaps they were influenced by an older student or teacher, or by a person they met who inspired them in some way. Maybe their experiences in a particular neighborhood have led them to work to change a community or help those less fortunate. Maybe their families changed with the addition of siblings or the separation of parents. Perhaps they have noticed their own physical, emotional, and intellectual changes over the past few years.

The poem that follows, "The Lost Girls," by Linda Hogan, is an example of observing the interior changes within one woman. The younger parts of the self are not completely lost, but seem to hover nearby, shadows of past life stages with whom the speaker of the poem may talk.

The Lost Girls

I don't remember when
the girl of myself turned her back
and walked away, that girl
whose thin arms
once held this body
and refused to work too hard
or listen in school,
said the hell then
and turned, that dark child,
that laugher and weeper
without shame, who turned
and skipped away.

And that other one
gone from me
and me
not even starting to knot
in vein or joint,
that curving girl
I loved to love with,
who danced away
the leather of red high heels
and thin legs, dancing like stopping
would mean the end of the world
and it does.

We go on
or we don't,
knowing about our inner women
and when they left us
like we were bad mothers or lovers
who wronged ourselves.

Some days it seems
one of them is watching, a shadow
at the edge of woods
with loose hair
clear down the back
and arms with dark moles
crossed before the dress I made

with my two red hands.
You there, girl, take my calloused hand.
I'm going to laugh and weep tonight,
quit all my jobs and I mean it this time,
do you believe me? I'm going to
put on those dancing shoes
and move till I can't stand
it anymore,
then touch myself clear down
to the sole of each sweet foot. That's all
the words I need,
not poems, not that talking mother
I was with milk and stories
peeking in at night,
but that lover of the moon
dancing outside when no one looks,
all right, then, even when they do,
and kissing each leaf of trees and squash,
and loving all the girls and women
I have always been.

— *Linda Hogan*

The transformation of child to adult is often surprising and even terrifying, as well as a time of unforeseen potential. In Elizabeth McKim's poem "Hips," the poet addresses her hips at a time they seem to be changing, taking on a new form.

Hips

you grew wings
I never wanted
when all the rest
of me was skinny
as a birch tree
you hummed
indecently under
grey flannel skirts
ma chose 2 sizes too big

you itched to take off
lisped vague pink lullabies
through the long adolescence
obsolescence you wanted something
beautiful / you wanted something
shining / you wanted something
circular / you wanted something
rising / you wanted something

surprising / you wanted
something / *singular*
immeasurable / and *immensely*
wise

— *Elizabeth McKim*

In the next poem, Rita Dove transforms the young girl into an adolescent through physical changes, the textures and smells of teenage dresses and cosmetics. The poet evokes the emerging young woman's fantasy about how her loved one will arrive. Yet this poem is framed by the inference that the father has left and the dream that the father returns as the daughter reaches womanhood.

Adolescence—III

With Dad gone, Mom and I worked
The dusky rows of tomatoes.
As they glowed orange in sunlight
And rotted in shadows, I too
Grew orange and softer, swelling out
Starched cotton slips.

The texture of twilight made me think of
Lengths of Dotted Swiss. In my room
I wrapped scarred knees in dresses
That once went to big-band dances;
I baptized my earlobes with rosewater.

Along the window sill, the lipstick stubs
Glittered in their steel shells.

Looking out at the rows of clay
And chicken manure, I dreamed how it
   would happen:
He would meet me by the blue spruce,
A carnation over his heart, saying,
"I have come for you, madam;
I have loved you in my dreams."
At his touch, the scabs would fall away.
Over his shoulder, I see my father coming
   toward us:
He carries his tears in a bowl,
And blood hangs in the pine-soaked air.

— *Rita Dove*

In "The Blue Dress," Sharon Olds uses the object, a blue dress, to reveal complex relationships in the speaker's family after her parents are divorced. The blue dress allows the speaker to explore her own ambivalences and necessary mythologies. The acute use of sense imagery allows the intense feelings in the poem to be revealed without melodrama or self-pity.

The Blue Dress

The first November after the divorce
there was a box from my father on my
birthday—no card, but a
big box from Hink's, the dark
department store with a balcony and
mahogany rail around the balcony, you could
stand and press your forehead against it
until you could almost feel the dense
grain of the wood, and stare down
into the rows and rows of camisoles
petticoats, bras, as if looking down
into the lives of women. The box
was from there, he had braved that place for me
the way he had entered my mother once
to get me out. I opened the box—I had
never had a present from him—
and there was a blue shirtwaist dress
blue as the side of a blue teal
disguised to go in safety on the steel-blue water.
I put it on, a perfect fit,
I liked that it was not too sexy, just a
blue dress for a 14-year-old daughter the way
Clark Kent's suit was just a plain suit for a
reporter, but I
felt the weave of that mercerized Indian Head
cotton against the skin of my upper arms and my
wide thin back and especially the skin of my
ribs under those new breasts I had
raised in the night like earthworks in
commemoration of his name.
A year later, during a fight about
just how awful my father had been,
my mother said he had not picked out the dress,
just told her to get something not too expensive,
and then had not even sent a check for it,
that's the kind of man he was. So I
never wore it again in her sight
but when I went away to boarding school I
wore it all the time there,
loving the feel of it, just
casually mentioning sometimes it was a gift

from my father,
wanting in those days to appear to have something
whether it was true or a lie, I didn't care, just to have something.

— Sharon Olds

Ask your students to compare these last two poems. They both deal with separation, the complexity of feelings toward parents, and a child's emergence into adolescence. Both poems use clothing as a central image. Is there some object or place in your students' lives that they can associate with ambivalent feelings or changes in relationships?

Poetry Exercise #3

Consider the important changes that have occurred in your life. Choose one you would like to explore in a poem. Is there metaphoric language you might use to help you avoid writing in abstractions? How did the change affect your life? You might address the lost part of you or the new part of you. You may choose one central image to bind together the feelings of the speaker. Remember vivid sense images will re-create your experience for the reader. Finish a draft. Does the poem allow you to remember your past life in a new way ?

Student Examples

Watching Changes Through a Lens

I watch the people around me.
I watch them change and move.
They all choose different paths.
Changing in their own way;
I watch mistakes and victories.

I see people trying too hard to change
as everyone else does.
I see some get caught
in a flow of people.

Being drowned in them as
if they were water.
Being carried away in their current.
I see others being left behind.

Sometimes I look back to me.
I look back,
Seeing how I have
changed in the years
Remembering all my mistakes
and victories.
Focusing my lens on me.

Everyone around me changing
Growing out of things and
people like clothes.
Trying to find their own
personality.

I watch my family change.
They grow out of things too.
As if they were an old
pair of jeans.
Finally deciding to go
and buy a new pair.

— Sarah Kassler

Johnny Was a Rebel

Johnny was a rebel
Since the day he was born.
You would have seen him
born feet first as he kicked and screamed.
You should have seen his parents
they just stood there and beamed.

It really started when he was five,
his parents gave him some scissors to play with.
You know, "Little Johnny be an artist."

They left him in his room,
he looked at the scissors,
he looked in the mirror.
What he saw was a cute face,
mounds of hair and perfectly straight teeth.
But his eyes had a space
They were unfilled.

Because although only five,
He had no purpose to his life.

So he said, "No more cute talk,
No more teddies,
I'm getting a Mohawk."
So he took his scissors
in his hand,
started cuttin' and thought
"my that looks grand."

His parents were terrified,
but Johnny was thrilled,
He had a good laugh
and the void was filled.

It went on for some years,
Johnny doing this,
Johnny doing that.
His parents were worried,
They dragged him to shrinks,
They tried to help,
get out the kinks.
But to no avail.

As far as he was concerned,
He was just having a laugh.

Then one day
When he was thirteen,
A realization hit him,
He looked into his mother's eyes
And saw what he had done
All he could say was,
Sorry, I was just having fun.

— *Patrick Doyle*

Queen

Why was I the one chosen
To become the queen bee?
I did nothing to deserve it,
At least nothing I could see.

All the others worked so hard
To earn the noble name.
Not to say I didn't try,
But my attempts were all so lame.

All of that is behind me now.
My fellow bees I must serve.
But how do they expect me to perform,
When I possess a power I don't deserve?

Now I feel the pressure mounting.
With all my fears growing strong.
All the younger ones look up to me,
And I'm afraid of doing wrong.

Why was I the one chosen
To become the queen bee?
I did nothing to deserve it,
At least nothing I could see.

— *Andy Katz-Mayfield*

Fourteen Year Oxymoron

To be fourteen is to be old and young at the same
time. It is a time of clear confusion and happy
sadness. It is a dream in reality. Oh! This age!
Sane craziness, right wrongness, pleasurable
pain. How short and long it is. When I am older
I know I will think those were the awfully
good times.

— *Sally Curcio*

Pensamientos / On Graduating

El día se acerca cuando tenemos que salir
    The day draws near when we must leave
y nunca podemos olvidar
    and we'll never forget
los días de felicidad
    the days of happiness
las sonrisas
    the smiles
las lágrimas . . .
    the tears
Pero ahora pensamos en el futuro
    But now we think about the future
queremos saludar lo nuevo
    we want to greet the new
sin perder lo viejo . . . y
    without losing the old . . . and
por eso decimos hasta luego
    that's why we say till then . . .
nunca decimos adiós . . .
    we'll never say goodbye

— *La clase de español grado ocho
Eighth-grade Spanish class*

Adolescence

Adolescence is tough.
Dealing with adolescence is a big job.
It's even harder for me
Because I have Apert's Syndrome to deal with.
Apert's Syndrome is a job in itself.
Day after day I always have to deal with
    adolescence.
Oh, it is such a job!
I better go now; I need to continue dealing
    with adolescence.

— Christopher Metafora

Lemon

They try to tell me I'm not what I think
They dye me and feed me full of their things.
Conform me.
    I am myself.
    I am fresh and sunny.
    Me.

They take me and reap me. Stamp me.
    Sun Kissed.

They use my juice. Squeeze my life out of me.
They take my scent to clean dishes and make
    hands softer.
They use my seeds to grow more.
They throw away my skin, my shell.
    Nothing left.

      I want to peel my skin off and show you
      the sun!

Well damn you. Yes you
I want you to see me.
You don't know me.
Don't say I'm fake.
I'm not unreal.
I am me.

— Amy Rosen

The River

A dry pit with rocks,
like the egg waiting for the sperm,
to give it life.

Rain drops fall,
like the unborn embryo,
in the mother's womb.

It starts to flow,
and the baby is born.

Overflowing,
like the teenage year,
of life.

In time, the sun dries up
the overflow of the river,
and we mature into middle age.

The river is drying up now,
only a few drops left,
our golden years.

It's dried up now,
but the rainy season,
will come again, the river waits,
with eagerness for the
rebirth.

— Edward Levitan

Emerging

The shine,
The yellow
The golden
is rising
Can this be
The Beginning?
My shining
My glow
My green
sight
so slowly
it opens
and buds into a spotted flower
I rise
my limbs
they open
the dried skin peels
and reveals
the shining flesh

that will take over.
The step into a wonderful vegetable
I hide,
and sleep,
and come out new
and blue
I step back,
one step

but a million steps
to all
in the wooden world . . .
My old world . . .
my wooden world
seems old
seems dark
seems gruesome.
And all who live there,
without stepping
into the light
into the glow
are still speaking
the wooden language
that I have left behind
long ago.

— *Lyn Bigelow*

4. To Arrive in a New World

In America, many students have experienced the dramatic changes of arriving from another country of birth. Many adolescents have powerful or painful memories of leaving a homeland, either willingly or under duress. Some families have planned for many years for such a change; others have to be ready to leave on a moment's notice. Some families have fled from violence or oppression, others have sought a better life for their families. But all of these students face vast economic, cultural, and social hardships. They have all left behind family and friends, familiar places and events, and a language which both holds and shapes their childhood memories. Maria Marrero, a Spanish bilingual teacher and poet, wrote this poem (for her newly arrived students) in the voice of her mother, who immigrated from Puerto Rico.

Where Are You From?

I am not from here.
I came a long time ago,
1947. When I arrived from
my island, it was
the 4th of July.
I forget the time.

I am not from here.
I came alone,
without children,
or husband,
without knowing English
I forgot the few
words I
was taught.

I am not from here.
My land is
humid and red,
The sun is hot
The rain splashes
on the tin roofs.
The land holds
the water and the plants
grow abundant.
I am not from here.

— *Maria Marrero*

In his poem "Borofels," Martín Espada describes the frustration of communication in a new language in which pronunciation is so different. Every second-language learner has probably experienced a similar incident.

Borofels
(for Sonia Nieto)
In Brooklyn, the mice were crazy
with courage, bony gray pickpockets
snatching crumbs from plates
at the table. The roaches
panicked in spirals on the floor,
or weaved down walls
for the sanctuary of cracked paint.
No heat, so the oven door drooped open
like an immigrant's surprise.

Sonia's mother was mute in English,
mouth chapped and coughing
without words to yell for heat.

But the neighbors spoke of Borofels:
Tell Borofels, and mice shrivel in traps,
roaches kick in poisoned heaps,
steam pipes bang so loud
that windows open in winter.

Sonia and her mother
sailed on a subway train rocking like a ship
desperate for light, then rose
in an untranslated territory
of Brooklyn. So Sonia translated:
"Where is Borofels?"
No one knew; the girl pinballed
by strangers in a hurry, hooded against frost
as mouths puffed quick clouds of denial.
Sonia saw the uniform then,
blue-coated trooper of the U.S. Mail,
and pleaded for Borofels.
His face, drowsing in bewilderment,
awoke with the gust
of what he suddenly understood
and he pointed down the street:
"You want
the Board of Health."

They could yell now
like banned poets
back from exile.

— *Martín Espada*

The poet Diana der Hovanessian explores the complexities of bridging two cultures and the identity questions which arise. She writes about her identity as an American with Armenian roots and the connection of her language to that issue. During this period of ethnic visibility and reidentification with ancestral roots, many second- and even third-generation Americans are examining their historical identities.

Two Voices

"Do you think of yourself as an Armenian? Or an American? Or hyphenated American?"

In what language do I pray?

Do I meditate in language?

In what language am I trying
to speak when I wake from dreams?

Do I think of myself as an American,
or simply as a woman when I wake?

Or do I think of the date and geography
I wake into, as woman?

Or do I think of myself in my clothes
getting wet walking in the rain?

Do I think velvet, or do I think skin?

Am I always conscious of genes and
heredity or merely how to cross my legs
at the angle like a New England lady?

In a storm do I think of lightning
striking? Or white knives dipped
into my great aunt's sisters'
sisters' blood?

Do I think of my grandfather telling
about the election at the time
of Teddy Roosevelt's third party,

and riding with Woodrow Wilson
in a Main Street parade
in Worcester?

Or do I think of my grandmother
at Ellis Island

or as an orphan in an Armenian village?

Or at a black stove in Worcester
baking blueberry pie for my grandfather
who preferred food he had grown
to like in lonely mill town
cafeterias while he studied
for night school?

Do I think of them as Armenian
or as tellers of the thousand and
one wonderful tales in two languages?

Do I think of myself as hyphenated?

No. Most of the time, even as you,
I forget labels.

Unless you cut me.

Then I look at the blood.
It speaks in Armenian.

— *Diana der Hovanessian*

Marilyn Chin, in her poem "Prelude," shows how her connection to her native country has become internalized. Her "heart is a house" in which her memories live and her love for her country is expressed through her poetry.

Prelude

To love your country
is to know its beginnings
not with the bald-face moon
or the complacent river—
but here within you.

Your heart is a house—
I/we are its inhabitants.
Although the country is lost
rivers and mountains remain.
And we shall always live
in this poetry that you love.

> — *Marilyn Chin*
> *for my mother, Wong Yuet Kuen*

Poetry Exercise #4

Try to recall the day you left the country of your birth. Perhaps there was a lot of waiting or traveling or danger involved. Or you may choose to write about the day you arrived in a new country—the United States of America or another country along the way. What images can you recall? what smells, shapes, colors, sounds, and tastes? Sense images will make your experience real to the reader. And if you can use similes or metaphors, they will enhance the reader's identification with your experience. What feelings did you have as you left or arrived? What or who were you leaving behind? What do you miss most about the country you left? What questions or expectations did you have about arriving in a new country? How do you feel being part of two cultures at once?

Of course, not all of your students are first-generation Americans. However, you will find that most of your students have grandparents or great-grandparents from foreign countries. You might ask them to write about an ancestor's first day in America.

Student Examples

Leaving Home

It isn't easy leaving home, leaving the only
    place you can truly love.
With words too great to explain,
I can only say,
The feeling I felt was greater than sorrow,
I felt like a butterfly,
Who didn't have wings.
On the plane, my memory grew dim,
And I shut out my surrounding,
Concentrating on home.
I shall forever remember my first hurdle,
One which I think will be the hardest of them all.
But to my children and grandchildren I will say,
"You never know when you are close, child.
    Never give up."
For it was these words of my great-grandmother,
which helped me get by.
And for my children, I hope it will be the same.

> — *Namrata Nanda Kumar*

El Mundo

Al llegar a otro mundo,
es como caer en un
hoyo negro todo sin
color y sin risas.

Es como buscar,
algo que no se
te ha perdido y que
nunca podrás
encontrarlo.

Cada día se va
y ni me doy cuenta,
como se va. Tal vez
se lo lleva el viento,
tal vez no.

> — *Piero Mercanti*

The World

To arrive in another world
is like falling into a
black hole all without
color and without laughter.

It's like looking
for something you
have not lost and
you will never find.

Every day passes
and I can hardly account
for it. Perhaps
the wind takes it,
perhaps not.

— *Piero Mercanti*
translated by Maria Marrero

My Homeland
(based on "Mi Patria," by Eva Margarita
Ortiz Platero")

My homeland, homeland of
my heart. I remember that time
when I left without your love.

Always I remember you when
I go walking. I remember
when I walked with disenchantment.

Oh, my homeland, my homeland
of my love I have always
loved you with all my heart.

I walk through the street thinking
of going there. But sometimes I think
that there I will find nothing.

My homeland, homeland of my heart.

— *Felix Alonzo*
translated by Maria Marrero

Ratana wrote this poem from a memory of
her escape as a very young child from Cambo-
dia across the border into a Thai refugee camp.

How I Made This Journey

How I made this journey
How I survive?
How I begin?
How I end?
Is still a question in my mind.
Three years into my life
it was a trip for my future,
the result would be my destiny.

It was rainy and wet
    the mud was knee high for my mom,
        for me it was over my head.
Everytime I fall
    because it was gloomy,
        the fullness of the forest
looked huge and monstrous
    like beasts were looming
        over me,
our pace of running
    was fast and moving.

All night
    all day
        we move
            with a rush
then suddenly
    like a curtain opening
        there beyond the trees
a group of blue tents stood
    the mere sight of it
        made our hearts hammer
It's like we've arrived in Heaven
    instead of just a camp site.

— *Ratana Tyriebe*

**Leaving Latin America—
Waiting in Caracas**

The dark wooden floor
feels cold and prickly
against my bottom.
I stare at Maria,
the only doll I brought with me,
through blurry tears
that flood my eyes.
A single tear spills over,
runs salty down my face,
and makes a little dark spot
right above her belly button,
on her favorite dress,
embroidered at the rim
with dancing teddies,
yellow silk as soft
as my own Mummy's cheek.
I don't know anything about this room,
except that it is big and white,
and that though I'm in it,
it's still not mine.
I miss the cozy hug of my old room.
I have no stuffed friends on a comfy bed,
no smiling stickers on the closet door.
In this box of faceless walls
whose arms are cold and frightening.
I haven't told the corners any secrets yet,
and I can tell the floor here
would get upset
if I rolled around or stomped on it.
So I just sit here,
My blue pallid skirt draping over my legs,
lonely in this empty room,
and quietly I mother my Maria.

— *Florencia Halperin*

5. CHOOSING THE FIRST LANGUAGE: NOTES FOR SECOND-LANGUAGE LEARNERS

Cultural Connection to Poetry

Growing numbers of our students come from backgrounds where poetry is an integral part of the culture. Hispanic, Russian, and Asian students often feel a great comfort in the expressive mode of poetry even before they have a facility with English. When students come from a culture where poetry is held in esteem and poetic thinking is as valued as logical thinking, then we must respect and build on these values. (Such unifying themes as family, environment, memory, and dream connect the experiences and cultures of our students.) If you can assure your students that you value their expression in their first language as much as their growing skills in their new language, they will be willing to take risks, speak honestly, and write from their heart.

Reading Poems in the First Language

One way to do this is to make available poetry in the first languages of your students, even if you can't read the poems. They may be willing to bring in poetry books from home. Ask them to choose a poem to read to the class. You can encourage your students to listen to the music of the language rather than the content. It's valuable to make a cassette tape of students reading in different languages, a festival of poetry from various nations.

Writing Poetry in the First Language

It is also worthwhile to encourage new students to write poems in their first languages, where the writer can hear the music and subtle meanings of each word. Language, itself, is structured in ways that affect how people think and feel. For example, the vocabulary and rituals of tribal cultures both reflect and shape the values and behavior of members of those cultures. Tribal beliefs in the unity of all things in the universe, and tribal respect for the earth and the natural forces that provide food and shelter are evident in language; the words and phrases shape the thought and feeling of each succeeding generation. In China, where family and ancestors are a central value, every individual member of a family has a specific term; for example, there is a word that means "the son of my uncle on my mother's side." In English, these terms are sometimes ambiguous. It is quite hard for a young student to express an exact feeling or value in a new language that may not have a corresponding word. Taking on the vocabulary of a new language can blur the boundaries of a person's identity.

What We Lose in Translation

In some languages, especially Russian and Spanish, the use of regular rhyme and meter dominates most published poetry, whereas in English, many freer (open) forms have been explored. Even if you don't speak the first languages of your students, you can tell by listening to a poem if it includes rhyme and a predictable meter. In Spanish, French, Italian, Portuguese, Hebrew, Arabic, and Russian, so many word endings are similar that language resonates strongly throughout poems in these languages and rhyming is much easier than in English. Listen carefully for cadence, music, rhyme, and rhythm. You can respond to these important aspects of the student's poem. If you have no one in your school who can translate the poem, ask a parent or put a notice in the school or community paper for a person who may be able to assist. A nearby university or religious center may be able to offer some leads.

Because of the importance of exact meaning, nuance, and connotation in poetry, our colleague Maria Marrero also gives her students the choice of using words from both English and Spanish in their poems until they feel secure in their new language. Many teachers follow this approach, which allows students to achieve mastery in a language appropriate to their age level even while they struggle to improve their English.

Poetry reading and writing seem to motivate second-language learners to share their first language and push forward in their English. Poetry is so deeply connected to culture, memory, dream, and spirituality that it transcends the barriers of language. Second-language students are eager and able to read published poems and their own original poems in both their first and second languages. In some cases, poetry opens the gate of thought and feeling, allowing students to feel less disoriented and isolated. Engagement with poetry validates the loss of a homeland and family and friends left behind. It sharpens the images of special places and people and moments of change. It documents the challenge of understanding a new culture and the hardship and effort that involves. Poetry is at the intersection of experience and response, rational thought and intuitive emotion, past and present, family and culture.

Chapter 5

Family and Relationships

Introduction

Relations among family members or between generations, friends, or two people in love are filled with emotions of every extreme. It is difficult to write about family and love relationships because it is hard to get enough distance. There is a danger of becoming too abstract or too clichéd. Writers employ techniques such as sense images, simile, metaphor, symbols, hyperbole, and apostrophe (address) to avoid abstraction and to allow the reader to enter the intimacy of a relationship.

Poems for Discussion

1. The Chinese Checker Players

When I was six years old
I played Chinese checkers
    with a woman
Who was ninety-three years old.
She lived by herself
in an apartment down the hall
    from ours.
    We played Chinese checkers
every Monday and Thursday nights.
While we played she usually talked
about her husband
who had been dead for seventy years,
and we drank tea and ate cookies
    and cheated.

                — *Richard Brautigan*

2. My Daughter Approaches Adolescence

You dance
on the dizzy edge of things
already you dream departure
as years ago
I dreamed divorce

    When I was where
    you are
    my momma said
    go slow
    she said
    the water has holes in it
    and the fish fall through
    she said
    no one should swim—
    not now
    with the sun on the water

Little guest of the garden
My brown and downy mouse
I know you can swim

I remember when you came to me
from the watery place
and all I could do
was get out of your way
give you up
to the pale room
and the gloved hands

    And now you will swim
    Through coves and bays and open seas
    You will wear water proudly
    And I like a well-used anchor will bear
        witness to your shining tides.

                — *Elizabeth McKim*

3. Harriet

Harriet there was always somebody calling
   us crazy
or mean or stuck-up or evil or black
or black
and we were
nappy girls quick as cuttlefish
scurrying for cover
trying to speak trying to speak
trying to speak
the pain in each other's mouths
until we learned
on the edge of a lash
or a tongue
on the edge of the other's betrayal
that respect
meant keeping our distance
in silence
averting our eyes
from each other's face in the street
from the beautiful dark mouth
and cautious familiar eyes
passing alone.

I remember you Harriet
before we were broken apart
we dreamed the crossed swords
or warrior queens
while we avoided each other's eyes
and we learned to know lonely
as the earth learns to know dead
Harriet Harriet
what name shall we call our selves now
our mother is gone?

                — *Audre Lorde*

4. Oranges

The first time I walked
With a girl, I was twelve,
Cold, and weighted down
With two oranges in my jacket.
December. Frost cracking
Beneath my steps, my breath
Before me, then gone,
As I walked toward
Her house, the one whose
Porch light burned yellow

Night and day, in any weather.
A dog barked at me, until
She came out pulling
At her gloves, face bright
With rouge. I smiled,
Touched her shoulder, and led
Her down the street, across
A used car lot and a line
Of newly planted trees,
Until we were breathing
Before a drugstore. We
Entered, the tiny bell
Bringing a saleslady
Down a narrow aisle of goods.
I turned to the candies
Tiered like bleachers
And asked what she wanted—
Light in her eyes, a smile
Starting at the corners
Of her mouth. I fingered
A nickel in my pocket,
And when she lifted a chocolate
That cost a dime,
I didn't say anything.
I took the nickel from
My pocket, then an orange,
And set them quietly on
The counter. When I looked up,
The lady's eyes met mine,
And held them, knowing
Very well what it was all
About.
              Outside,
A few cars hissing past,
Fog hanging like old
Coats between the trees.
I took my girl's hand
In mine for two blocks,
Then released it to let
Her unwrap the chocolate.
I peeled my orange
That was so bright against
The gray of December
That, from some distance,
Someone might have thought
I was making a fire in my hands.

                — *Gary Soto*

5. Sonnet 116

Let me not to the marriage of true minds
Admit impediments. Love is not love
Which alters when it alteration finds
Or bends with the remover to remove.
O, no! It is an ever-fixed mark
That looks on tempests and is never shaken.
It is the star to every wand'ring bark,
Whose worth's unknown, although his heighth be taken.
Love's not Time's fool, though rosy lips and cheeks
Within his bending sickle's compass come.
Love alters not with his brief hours and weeks,
But bears it out even to the edge of doom.
      If this be error and upon me proved,
      I never writ, nor no man ever loved.

               — *William Shakespeare*

6. somewhere i have never travelled

somewhere i have never travelled, gladly beyond
any experience, your eyes have their silence:
in your most frail gesture are things which enclose me,
or which i cannot touch because they are too near

your slightest look easily will unclose me
though i have closed myself as fingers,
you open always petal by petal myself as Spring opens
(touching skillfully, mysteriously) her first rose

or if your wish be to close me, i and
my life will shut very beautifully, suddenly,
as when the heart of this flower imagines
the snow carefully everywhere descending;

nothing which we are to perceive in this world equals
the power of your intense fragility: whose texture
compels me with the colour of its countries,
rendering death and forever with each breathing

(i do not know what it is about you that closes
and opens; only something in me understands
the voice of your eyes is deeper than all roses)
nobody, not even the rain, has such small hands

               — *e.e. cummings*

7. Do Not Go Gentle into That Good Night

Do not go gentle into that good night,
Old age should burn and rave at close of day;
Rage, rage against the dying of the light.

Though wise men at their end know dark is right,
Because their words had forked no lightning they
Do not go gentle into that good night.

Good men, the last wave by, crying how bright
Their frail deeds might have danced in a green bay,
Rage, rage against the dying of the light.

Wild men who caught and sang the sun in flight,
And learn, too late, they grieved it on its way,
Do not go gentle into that good night.

Grave men, near death, who see with blinding sight
Blind eyes could blaze like meteors and be gay,
Rage, rage against the dying of the light.

And you, my father, there on the sad height,
Curse, bless, me now with your fierce tears, I pray.
Do not go gentle into that good night.
Rage, rage against the dying of the light.

— Dylan Thomas

Questions for Discussion and Analysis

1. In Richard Brautigan's "The Chinese Checker Players," how would you characterize the relationship between these two neighbors? What do we learn about each character? How does Brautigan use time (six years, ninety-three years, seventy years, Monday/Thursday nights), to both separate and unite his characters? What is the tone of the poem? (Tone is the author's attitude toward a subject—ironic, serious, or humorous—not to be confused with mood, which is the climate of feeling or atmosphere created by the author. Tone can be conveyed through the author's specific choice of words and details, portraying character, describing settings, and elaborating on events.) Why does the narrator conclude by mentioning tea, cookies, and cheating?

2. In Elizabeth McKim's poem "My Daughter Approaches Adolescence," who is talking to whom? What memories does the mother recall to help her cope with the changes her daughter is going through? Show how each stanza in McKim's poem represents a different time period. How many times is a water image alluded to in this poem, and what does it represent in each instance? What language adds to the dreamlike tone of the poem?

3. Who is Harriet in the poem "Harriet" by Audre Lorde? (This name carries considerable historic weight.) A wide range of emotions surface in this poem, including defensiveness, anger, sassiness, longing, a desire for comfort and forbidden love, loneliness, pain, and aloofness. What sections of the poem convey these emotions? How does Lorde's repetitive language hold the reader's attention? How do these repetitions in

words, phrases, or sentence structure build rhythm?

4. Gary Soto's poem "Oranges" evokes strong images and contrasts of light and color, beginning with the title itself. Identify the different colors used by Soto, and discuss your personal associations with them. How does the saleslady conspire with the twelve-year-old boy to make this first-time experience so unique and memorable? Why does "a fire in my hands" work so well as a closing metaphor?

5. In William Shakespeare's "Sonnet 116," what is the overall theme of the poem? Where does Shakespeare use elevated language? hyperbole? What is the tone of this poem? Is it ambiguous? What language and image support your point of view? Can you identify the rhyme scheme of this sonnet? This particular rhyme scheme is called a Shakespearean sonnet. Are there any slant rhymes in the sonnet? Can you scan the poem? Where does it differ from perfect iambic pentameter (-/-/-/-/-/)? Why did Shakespeare deviate from a sonnet's rhythm? (Refer to glossary.)

6. In "somewhere i have never travelled," E.E. Cummings uses spring and nature to represent both his loved one and the love he feels. Yet, he states that this is an inadequate expression of his feelings. Show how Cummings uses nature to express love. Look at the following phrases: "somewhere I have never travelled," "I cannot touch because they are too near," "the power of your intense fragility." What do these phrases allude to? How do they show the narrator's passion? How is the language contradictory? Compare "somewhere . . ." to the Shakespearean sonnet. How does the tone of the Cummings poem differ from that of Shakespeare's love sonnet? What techniques do both of these writers use to express love?

7. In "Do Not Go Gentle into That Good Night," by Dylan Thomas, what metaphors are used to represent death? Through what four examples does the poet implore his father to "not go gentle into that good night"? What exactly is the narrator asking from his father? (See last verse.) Reread the poem and identify the rhyme scheme and the metrics. (*Note:* This meter is iambic pentameter.) Do you find lines from stanza one repeated throughout the poem? (Indicate which lines are repeated and where.) This particular meter, rhyme scheme, and repetitive pattern are elements of the *villanelle,* a complicated and rigorous Renaissance form adapted by the French poet Jean Passerat. Can you speculate on why Thomas chose the villanelle form for this particular subject?

Bibliography of Additional Poems

"Driving My Parents Home at Christmas," Robert Bly
"Now!" Robert Browning
"Brown Boy to Brown Girl," Countee Cullen
"Little Brown Baby," Paul Laurence Dunbar
"At Night," Richard Eberhart
"My Sister Jane," Ted Hughes
"I Love You in Caves and Meadows," David Ignatow
Strings: A Gathering of Family Poems, Paul Janeczko, ed.
"I Want to Die While You Love Me," Georgia Douglas Johnson
"The Passionate Shepherd to His Love," Christopher Marlowe
"To His Coy Mistress," Andrew Marvell
"Elegy for My Father," Howard Moss
"Mi Hijo," Pablo Neruda
"A Birthday" and "Echo," Christina Rossetti
"To Atthis," Sappho
"My Little Stringbean," Anne Sexton
"At My Father's House," Nancy Travis
"Did This Happen to Your Mother? Did Your Sister Throw Up a Lot?" Alice Walker
"Lineage," Margaret Walker
"A Dance for Ma Rainey," Al Young

Writing Exercises

1. FAMILY PORTRAITS IN WORDS

The writer must learn to focus almost like a camera, framing a shot in order to capture a specific moment in a person's life that characterizes and re-creates the whole person. Senses and emotions surrounding that moment give a more profound dimension to the subject of the poem.

The language in Robert Hayden's "Those Winter Sundays" is so vivid that it is easy for the reader to visualize the father's "cracked hands," the son's polished shoes, and to hear "the cold splintering" of wood. In this portrait, the writer comes to understand the strengths of his father through the quiet sacrifice that man made for his family. For the son looking back on his childhood, it is his father's love on those winter Sundays that transcends the cold, harsh, and austere atmosphere of his home.

Those Winter Sundays

Sundays too my father got up early
and put his clothes on in the blueblack cold,
then with cracked hands that ached
from labor in the weekday weather made
banked fires blaze. No one ever thanked him.

I'd wake and hear the cold splintering, breaking.
When the rooms were warm, he'd call,
and slowly I would rise and dress,
fearing the chronic angers of that house,

Speaking indifferently to him,
who had driven out the cold
and polished my good shoes as well.
What did I know, what did I know
of love's austere and lonely offices?

— *Robert Hayden*

In "Family Tree," Kate Rushin speaks in the vernacular about her grandmother. This poem dwells less on physical detail than on the actions of the grandmother.

The grandmother means to pass down a value system through specific object symbols. What unique traits or interests about your own grandparents have made an impression on you or changed how you function in your community?

Family Tree

I come from
A long line of
Uppity Irate Black Women
Although they were
Church People
And I'm the only one
Who drinks and cusses
When they got on the warpath
let me tell you
They had no match
You think I'm bold
Imagine my grandmother Addie
Raising her umpteen children
During the Depression
Imagine the audacity of
This woman who only
Went to the third grade
Joining The-Book-Of-The-Month Club
She gave me a six volumes set of
The World's Best Poetry
When I was seven years old
When I was nine
My grandmother sent
A coupon and one dollar to
Nabisco Shredded Wheat
They sent her a knife
And fork and spoon
She kept them in a yellow
Envelope in the dish closet drawer
She would say they were for me
For when I went away to college
I didn't know what it meant exactly
But I would open the drawer
And look at them
And it made me feel
Real Good
And you ask me how come
I think I'm so cute
Nowadays

I cultivate
Being Uppity
It's something
My Grandmom taught me
It's about time I learned
My lesson.

— *Kate Rushin*

Poetry Exercise #1

Choose a person in your family or someone you know well and create a portrait
with words. Choose a setting in which to
place this person, such as at home, at school,
at play, or in the context of a social event or
family affair. This setting becomes the background to your family portrait and helps
bring the portrait to life. Senses, similes,
metaphors will bring color, texture, and
style to your portrait. You might try a poem
which represents a teenage point of view
in coping with parents. What central image
would you choose?

Student Examples

La Madre,

La persona mas dulce y comprensiva
que lo que puede ser un dulce
su mirada dulce y penetrante como
la de un aguila, su corazón
fuerte y vigoroso capas de soportar
cualquier dolor. Si yo tuviese poder
alguno buscaría en todo el universo
alguna estrella que pudiese significar
su gran amor. Cada vez que te veo en
   alguna foto
me recuerdo de aquellos días en que tu y yo nos
acostabamos tardicimo estudiando matemáticas,
cada vez que me veo en un espejo
se me refleja tu dulce cara y me trae una
gran sensación de tristeza el no poderte
tener aquí conmigo.

— *Rafael Angarita*

The Mother,

The sweetest, most understanding person,
like what a candy can be,
her sweet and penetrating glance like
that of an eagle, her heart
strong and vigorous capable of supporting
any pain. If I had any power
I would search the universe
for some star that could signify
her great love.
               Every time I see you in a photo
I remember the days when you and I
would go to bed so late studying math,
every time I see myself in the mirror,
your sweet face is reflected and it brings me
a great sensation of sadness to not have
you here with me.

— *Rafael Angarita*
translated by Maria Marrero

Morning Treat

Tender eyes blink open
In the early morn.
The soft padding of bare feet
Down a warm, furry carpeted staircase.
The clock's tick is heard throughout the house
As an early dawn silence rests peacefully
Like a warm blanket
Upon the household.
The next step brings warm, tiny toes
To a chilling, square patterned kitchen floor.
The kitchen: warm sunlight streams in,
And the quiet hum of the fridge is constant.
A hunger and curiousness
Starts the innocent mind thinking.
There sits a tasty, vulnerable watermelon.
Pudgy, clumsy hands grip the melon.
Soft lips and tiny teeth sink into it.
Sweet, sticky juice drips down the chin
And onto the floor.
The soft clutter of seeds being deposited
On the kitchen floor.
A chew, a swallow, a little burp.
Satisfaction. Rest. Peace. A mess.
A look, a smile, a laugh.
Look what the baby has done now!
She says.

— *Ronny Weiner*

Such a Sweet Old Man

Such a sweet old man,
Walking on the ground,
Handing me balloons,
Shivering all the while.

Such a tired old man,
Lying in his white bed,
Not knowing who I am,
Eating from a needle and a tube.

Such a clean old man,
Lying all dressed up,
In a satin bed,
With a pillow under his head.

Soon loud guns,
Will shoot through the air,
Ringing in my ears,
Clashing with my tears.

My great-grandfather,
He is thrown to the wind.
His ashes will live on,
Floating on the bay,
Not knowing where they are.

Such a sweet old man,
He is gone from my life,
Gone forever,
But not from my mind.

— *Kathleen Maeve Caulfield*

Father

The one gets half credit
For my life.
The one sends me to school
In winter times.
The one gives me money
For school lunches.
The one comes back home late
Almost every other night.
The one never realized I got
My ears pierced.
The one cares more about my grades
Than how I feel.

But, he is the one that loves me more
Than anything in the world.

— *Pei Jiin*

My Mother

The sweet woman we all want to have,
Her smiles, hugs that come deep within
    her heart,
The twinkle in her eye when she picked you
up.
Her voice to charm you when she sang a lull-
aby. Who sat and watched your little head,
When you were sleeping in your sweet,
    soft, bed.
Who taught you how to talk and pray,
To walk in wisdom every day.
Who was the woman who rocked us
when we cried? Our Mother.
The memories come back to our head.
As she falls into a deep long rest.
The memories of the love we share
Come back as we are proud to say
That woman was my mother.

— *Leo Diaz*

Why Did He Have to Be This Way?

Didn't know my grandpa much,
Searching back through memories.
He gripped his cane,
stared into the deep black sky
suddenly then turning to night
like his family.
Deep in mysteries
Didn't know why?
Met him once
In my lifetime.
Acted like I was nothing,
like my brother was the world.
My parents say he was a good man.
Maybe in his special ways, he was.
His life faded away,
like leaving a cup of water
in the dry desert.
Seeing sadness,
in this old man's wrinkled face.
Why did he have to be this way?

— *Despina Felis*

2. REVEALING CONNECTIONS

To reveal the emotional connections between two people, poets may use an event and the specific details surrounding it to clarify the nature of the relationship. In the following poems, color, texture, temperature, taste, and snatches of conversation give an energy to the emotional exchange between the two parties in the poem. In David Huddle's "Icicle," the texture of "the soft pad of your lower lip" and the temperature of the "morning . . . cold, windy, bright as Russia" not only create a specific day, but also define a brittleness and pain between the writer and the brother he is addressing.

Icicle

I smacked you in the mouth for no good reason
except that the icicle had broken off
so easily and that it felt like a club
in my hand, and so I swung it, the soft
pad of your lower lip sprouting a drop,
then gushing a trail onto the snow even
though we both squeezed the place with
   our fingers
I'd give a lot not to be the swinger
of that icicle. I'd like another
morning just like that, cold, windy, and bright
as Russia, your glasses fogging up, your face
turning to me again. I tell you I might
help both our lives by changing that act to this,
by handing you the ice, a gift, my brother.

          — *David Huddle*

In "Family Picnic," Judith Steinbergh uses the simile "you gulp down the words like watermelon" to reflect the intense fascination the child holds toward the grandmother's stories.

Family Picnic

All yellow and pink, child
   you orbit my grandmother
      as if she were the sun.

She is so old
   she moves like a glacier, and you are
      the bell clear river that trails her.

Her creases map the century
   her tongue still touches a strange alphabet
      her heart slows down to a hibernating bear.

She tells you a story I have heard
   a thousand times and you gulp down
      the words like watermelon.

Holding her, you teeter over the grass
Holding you, she recrosses continents.

          — *Judith Steinbergh*

Li-Young Lee explores his cultural roots imagining specific places and weather through the songs of his mother and grandmother. The songs have the power to re-create the old country for him. The image of the waterlilies filling and spilling their rain resonates with the women's tears flowing even as they sing.

I Ask My Mother to Sing

She begins, and my grandmother joins her.
Mother and daughter sing like young girls.
If my father were alive, he would play
his accordion and sway like a boat.

I've never been in Peking, or the Summer Palace,
nor stood on the great Stone Boat to watch
the rain begin on Kuen Ming Lake, the picnickers
running away in the grass.

But I love to hear it sung;
how the waterlilies fill with rain until
they overturn, spilling water into water,
then rock back, and fill with more.

Both women have begun to cry.
But neither stops her song.

          — *Li-Young Lee*

Most of Sharon Olds's poem "The Race" describes an experience at the airport, but the frantic pace of the language and imagery such as "fish slipping upstream" and "planets in world orbits" convey a sense of the writer's desperation to see her father before he dies.

The Race

When I got to the airport I rushed up to the desk
and they told me the flight was canceled. The
    doctors had
said my father would not live through the night
and the flight was canceled. A young man with a
dark blond mustache told me
another airline had a non-stop
leaving in seven minutes—see that
elevator over there well go
down to the first floor, make a right you'll
see a yellow bus, get off at the
second Pan Am terminal—I
ran, I who have no sense of direction
raced exactly where he'd told me, like a fish
slipping upstream deftly against the
flow of the river. I jumped off that bus with my
heavy bags and ran, the bags
wagged me from side to side as if to
prove I was under the claims of the material, I
ran up to a man with a white flower on
    his breast,
I who always go to the end of the line, I said
Help me. He looked at my ticket, he said make a
left and then a right go up the moving stairs
    and then
run. I raced up the moving stairs
two at a time, at the top I saw the
long hollow corridor and
then I took a deep breath, I said
goodbye to my body, goodbye to comfort, I
used my legs and heart as if I would
gladly use them up for this, to
touch him again in this life. I ran and the
big heavy dark bags
banged me, wheeled and swam around me like
planets in world orbits—I have seen

pictures of women running down roads
    with their
belongings tied in black scarves
grasped in their fists, running under serious
gray historical skies—I blessed my
long legs he gave me, my strong
heart I abandoned to its own purpose, I
ran to Gate 17 and they were
just lifting the thick white
lozenge of the door to fit it into the
socket of the plane. Like the man who is not
too rich, I turned to the side and
slipped through the needle's eye, and then I
walked down the aisle toward my father. The
    jet was
full and people's hair was shining, they were
smiling, the interior of the plane was filled with a
mist of gold endorphin light,
I wept as people weep when they enter heaven,
in massive relief. We lifted up
gently from one tip of the continent and
did not stop until we set down lightly on the
other edge. I walked into his room and
watched his chest rise slowly and
sink again, all night
I watched him breathe.

— *Sharon Olds*

Poetry Exercise #2

Choose two people (one of them could be you) and portray their relationship. Use an event that is charged with emotion to focus on a specific aspect of the relationship. Be aware of how you want the reader to feel toward the people in the poem. Senses, similes, metaphors will root the abstract feelings in recognizable experiences for the reader.

Student Examples

Footprints

Friday

The young girl and the older man are together
They climb into the old rusty car
Their bags securely packed in the trunk
The girl feels excited
She shivers with the delight of going to
   Cape Cod
alone with her father.
They switch on the radio and listen to voices.
Some of his choice, which she doesn't like,
   but listens
to anyway.
And some of her choice, which he doesn't
   like, but
listens to anyway.
Neither of them complain.
They chatter about her brother
They chatter about her school work
They have no cares.

They speed by the other cars.
Finally, they arrive in the sandy, deserted
   parking lot
It is late in the season so they are alone.
They pluck their shoes off their feet and
scatter excitedly up over the hill.
The cold sand slips between their toes and adds
to their happiness.
The horizon comes into sight.
Millions of fiery colors fill the sky.

Now there are no Fridays together.
The girl cannot have a civilized conversation
with the man.
They are two completely different people.
Now when the girl walks on the beach.
She walks with her peers, forward.
Her footprints are lost with the other footprints.
There still are those many quarrels.
But lately they do not wash away so quickly.

— *Rachel Zindler*

Marriage

We finally decided to do it,
Marriage is a commitment.
Good times with our family,
Marriage is wonderful.
All these bills, bills, bills,
Marriage is a responsibility.
Questions, Questions, Questions,
Marriage is hardwork.
All these questions, bills, hardwork,
Marriage is not worth it.
I can't take this anymore
Marriage is over.
Divorce

— *Imara*

Un Recuerdo

En el fondo de su casa vive,
su espíritu en el silencio
con sus cosas y utensilios
en la oscura eternidad.
En la ventana,
sus vestidos vuelan sin cesar,
pero no se escapan no.
Se retienen,
no se quieren ir,
su estado los detiene
parece que recuerdan a mi abuela
   alegre, tradicional,
y su boca, chiquita como una almendra,
   sus ojos, negros como la mas oscura noche,
brillan sin cesar.
Con sus manos
trabajando sin cesar
trabajo contenta hasta su muerte.
Me contaron que cogió una tigresa y una
   serpiente.
La tigresa, amarilla como el sol con la noche
y la serpiente larga y gruesa.
Me gustaría haber estado alla, haber sido ella.
Tuvo hijos, todos fieles a su madre que fue
   su maestra.
Algunas veces, me arrepiento de haber
   nacido tan
pronto, pero no fue mi culpa.
   La vida es asi: INJUSTA.

— *Sandra Calderon*

A Memory

In the depths of her house lives
her spirit in silence with her belongings
in the eternal darkness.
In the window, her clothes float in the breeze
but they can't escape, no.
They are trapped,
They don't want to leave.
And it seems as though they
remember my grandmother,
her happy traditional ways,
her mouth, small like an almond,
her eyes, black, like the darkest night
shining ceaselessly.
Her hands always working,
working contentedly until her death.
They told me that she caught a tigress and
   a serpent.
The tigress, yellow like the sun with the night,
and the serpent heavy and thick.
I would like to have been there, to have been her.
She had sons, all faithful to their mother,
   their teacher.
Sometimes I regret having been born so late,
but the fault is not with me.
Life is that way: UNJUST!

— *Sandra Calderon*
translated by Maria Marrero

Through the Eyes of Two

To stand as young
So young
So innocent
through the eyes of
a child
a child unknowing
unaware
to escape the scene of a
harsh violence.
Down to the floor a loud
thud.
Being hurt even more
with the hand of the enemy
the mother so frail

so tender
thrown around in front
of her young.
I stand and watch but
what am I to do?
A tear escapes my eye.
Envy has never taken
part of my life
until now.
A lump in my heart
a stone as his
such times as now
a knife in my hand would please me.
But what was I to know
a child of two.
Torment has taken its toll?
and the enemy is gone.
Walk the floor almost slipping
on a blood spot
following it to
the bathroom
where she stands rinsing.
She takes me by the hand
whispers words to me.
My brother just in the other room
comes out.
Going through the doors of our apartment
now knowing that was
the last time. We approach
her mother's house.
We stay for a while.
In the morning
she's gone.

— *Evania L.*

3. POEMS OF ADDRESS

One way to bring a person into a poem
quickly and intimately is by using the form
of address. By speaking directly to people,
whether or not they are present, absent, or
deceased, the poet draws them into the poem
and suggests a close relationship. In "Family
Picnic" in the Revealing Connections section of
this chapter, poet Judith Steinbergh addresses
her daughter, but describes the relationship
between the daughter and the great-grand-

mother. Another poem, "Mother to Son," by Langston Hughes, conveys a feeling of both love and sorrow as the mother speaks directly to her son. Hughes was one of the first poets to explore spoken dialect in poems.

Mother to Son

Well, son, I'll tell you:
Life for me ain't been no crystal stair.
It's had tacks in it,
And splinters,
And boards torn up,
And places with no carpet on the floor—
Bare.
But all the time
I'se been a-climbin' on,
And reachin' landin's
And turnin' corners,
And sometimes goin' in the dark
Where there ain't been no light.
So, boy, don't you turn back.
Don't you set down on the steps
'Cause you find it's kinder hard.
Don't you fall now—
For I'se still goin', honey,
I'se still climbin',
And life for me ain't been no crystal stair.

— *Langston Hughes*

In "My Papa's Waltz," the poet confronts the father using the form of address, but his choice of a tight formal structure and rhyming quatrains enables him to keep some distance from the painful nature of the subject.

My Papa's Waltz

The whiskey on your breath
Could make a small boy dizzy;
But I hung on like death:
Such waltzing was not easy.

We romped until the pans
Slid from the kitchen shelf;
My mother's countenance
Could not unfrown itself.

The hand that held my wrist
Was battered on one knuckle;
And every step you missed
My right ear scraped a buckle.

You beat time on my head
With a palm caked hard by dirt,
Then waltzed me off to bed
Still clinging to your shirt.

— *Theodore Roethke*

The following poem of address from Mexico demonstrates the intimacy of the form. Each word and phrase, each metaphor conveys how much the mother treasures her daughter.

My Daughter

(extract)

My necklace of precious stones
    You are turquoise
    you are jade
    you are feather

You are my blood
you are my colour
you are my image

    listen my child
    understand my child

You are alive
you're born
    come close to me
    listen!

— *traditional Mexican*
translated by Toni de Gerez

Poetry Exercise #3

Try revising your poem from the Family Portraits exercise, transforming it into a poem of address to see how it affects the tone or impact on the reader. You may want to try writing a new poem, which addresses another person (a family member, friend, or historical figure), and imagine you are speaking directly to that person.

Student Examples

Growing Old Together

Growing old together
You look at me and I see wrinkles around
    your face
You tell me stories about when you were little
And you liked horses just like me
You look at me and I see legs honey and white
You touch my hand and I feel damp cold hands
I hear you talking in a rough voice
You can't run and play with me and skin your
    knee
Your hand rough and scaly
I'm growing old and so are you
But we can't stop time and let every one else
    grow old
We are growing old together.

            — *Pam*

What's the Matter with Me

(*the grandfather speaks*)

I am slowing down
like a wrinkled tortoise
walking down a long road.
You are speeding up
like a well-oiled train
that has no rust,
What's the matter with me?

You stand and run,
I sit and walk
I do whatever I want,
you can too.
I get tired and fussy
You wake up like a farmer
You don't complain
Yet we're both changing
What's the matter with me?

            — *Steven J. McCoy*

It's Your Mother Talking

It's your mother talking, can't you hear?
It's your mother talking about her heartache
    and tears.
It's your mother talking, oh, can't you hear?
It's your mother talking, but you live in fear.
It's your mother talking, why can't you hear?
It's your mother talking, listen to her tears.
It's your mother talking, her heart is
    pouring out.
It's your mother talking, listen and
you'll know what she's talking about.

            — *Lynn Wood*

4. FAMILY HEIRLOOMS

The connection between two generations, or the thread that runs through a family, can be conveyed in a poem by using an heirloom that symbolizes continuity. You can discuss with your students a wide range of heirlooms: objects of value, history, or nostalgia; recipes; songs, dances, or lullabies; family stories, rituals, or customs; books or photographs; physical appearance or temperament; a special talent for music, art, math, or language; a special name. In "Legacies," Nikki Giovanni writes about something that might be passed along from the grandmother to a granddaughter who resists receiving it.

Legacies

her grandmother called her from the playground
    "yes, ma'am"
      "i want chu to learn how to make rolls," said
      the old
woman proudly
but the little girl didn't want
to learn how because she knew
even if she couldn't say it that
that would mean when the old one died she
    would be less
dependent upon her spirit so
she said
    "i don't want to know how to make no rolls"

with the lips poked out
and the old woman wiped her hands on
her apron saying "lord
    these children"
and neither of them ever
said what they meant
and i guess nobody ever does

— *Nikki Giovanni*

Gail Harada describes the "old way" of celebrating the New Year. She uses sense images, foods, Japanese words, to help the reader who is new to such a ritual. Through her poem, she passes this custom down to future generations. She is the bridge between the old way and the new.

New Year

This is the old way,
the whole clan gathered,
the rice steaming over the charcoal.
the women in the room, talking,
a layer of potato starch on the table.

This is the old way,
the father watching his son lift the mallet,
pound the rice, pound mochi,
the children watching or playing,
the run of the dough to the women,
the rolling of the round cakes.

This is the old way,
eating ozoni, new year's soup:
mochi for longevity,
daikon, long white radish
rooted firmly like families;
eating burdock, also deeply rooted,
fish for general good luck,
the lotus root, wheel of life.

This is the old way, setting off firecrackers
to drive away evil spirits,
leaving the driveways red for good fortune.

The new year arrives,
deaf, smelling of gunpowder.

— *Gail Harada*

You may have a name that belonged to your father or grandfather or uncle. Part of your name may be from your mother or your aunt. You may have a name in English and another in Chinese or Hebrew. A name can carry a family history, a sense of pride. A family name can embrace a family's history and potential, its sorrows and strengths, its values and beliefs. Linda Hogan lets us see how a name could reveal stories of your grandparents, their hardships, their landscape, the complexities of a mixed marriage.

Song for My Name

Before sunrise
think of brushing out an old woman's
dark braids.
Think of your hands,
fingertips on the soft hair.

If you have this name,
your grandfather's dark hands
lead horses toward the wagon
and a cloud of dust follows,
ghost of silence.

That name is full of women
with black hair
and men with eyes like night.
It means no money
tomorrow.

Such a name my mother loves
while she works gently
in the small house.
She is a white dove
and in her own land
the mornings are pale,
birds sing into the white curtains
and show off their soft breasts.

If you have a name like this,
there's never enough water.
There is too much heat.
When lightning strikes, rain
refuses to follow.
It's my name,
that of a woman living
between the white moon
and the red sun, waiting to leave.
It's the name that goes with me
back to earth
no one else can touch.

— *Linda Hogan*

Poetry Exercise #4

Consider all of the objects, talents, customs, names, or family traits that have been passed along in your family. Choose one to tell us something about what you carry forward, what connects you to your past. In your poem, describe that heirloom using the appropriate sense images and similes or metaphors to clarify your subject. From whom does this heirloom come? What does it mean to you, where do you keep it, or how do you use it? Has it changed your life in any way? Do you think you might pass it on eventually?

If you cannot think of any quality, custom, or object passed down to you, you might consider something you value, such as an old teddy bear or a well-used hockey stick or a signed baseball. You might pass along such a treasure to one of your own children someday.

Student Examples

Both Steven and Marya chose the violin as a central image, a concrete object that symbolizes the abstract idea of family continuity. Steven begins by endowing music with broad and abstract qualities. He ends with "the song plays me," capturing perfectly how music from a loved one resonates in the body and mind of the one who receives it.

The Violin

Music is the sound of life,
enchantment and heritage,
I listen to the sounds of violin,
the one instrument that has changed
the way I feel.
My grandfather
had taught me to play,
At my grandfather's funeral,
I play the violin in despair,
this song I play is
the violin laying him to rest.
I mourn as I leave his grave,
playing the violin, giving him
a special goodbye.
As I get ready for bed,
I look out the window
staring at the sunset, hearing
the echo of my grandfather's
favorite song. The song plays me.

— *Steven J. McCoy*

Marya, on the other hand, moves toward greater abstraction as she approaches the end of her poem.

The Violin Circle

On its side
the violin lies waiting,
waiting to come alive again.
Its youthful player
who wove a timeless symphony
is gone now.
His instrument has fallen silent,
gathering dust
in a distant room.
Generations later
two gnarled hands
pass it lovingly
to a grandchild.
The youthful player
holds it gently once again,
touching old grooves
with infinite care.
Drawing her bow across the strings,
the child resumes the ageless symphony,
knitting together past and present
in the harmony of sound.

— *Marya J. Cohen*

My Recipe Box

Each one is a story waiting to be told.
In between the eggs and butter is my great grandmother's soul.
Next to the half cup milk are Grandmother's hazel eyes.
They shine out at me like stars filled with love and dreams.
From inside the apple dusted with cinnamon my mother smiles at me.
We call to each other through the haze of the steamy, living, kitchen.
We look at each other from behind the Kosher oven door, trapped by time and tradition.
I stir the batter, one hundred strokes.
I inhale the light gooey smell.
I feel my family.
And as I cut the completed hot cake I find myself,
as I will someday find my children in the walnuts and chocolate chips I sprinkled on the top.
We have been stirred with a blade of steel.
We have been grated by gnarled fingers that are somehow smooth.
We have been smooshed and loved in countless children's palms as we learned.
But we have always been kneaded by hands that love and live.
And we are still whole.
And my recipe box is still complete, continuing and ageless
And each recipe is a story waiting to be told.

— *Jennie Emma Weinberger*

Here, Jason gives the idea of passing on family talents a twist by choosing a trait of questionable value.

Mr. Fixit

Of all the things that I could have
inherited from my wonderful father,
I'm glad that one of them is
not the illustrious malaise
of Mr. Fixit.
Fixing anything and everything that
is broken and never quite finishing,
is a result of the disease that
he has worked to perfection
many times over.
Under the roofs, fixed uncountable times,
using the pipes replaced by my father,
who works like a beaver, then
puts off finishing it
like a grasshopper.
Although we beg and plead, he never
listens to reason.

And never allows us to pick up
the phone and dial the little used number
of the repairman.
Luckily, I do not have it,
I leave things as they are

But the thing I worry about is not
that I'm going to get it later, but
what about my children?

— *Jason Wright*

In reflecting on her family name, Chandra has borrowed, perhaps unconsciously, the form and mystery of Emily Dickinson. The poem breaks out of this form the way an adolescent would pull away from her family to establish her own independence and voice.

There Is No Secret

There is no secret to my name,
No myth that I should hide,
There is no password or code,
It's not as solid as ice,

It doesn't drift upon the wind,
Or float the sea with ease,
There is no rhyme or reason,
no melody to sing.

It does not give me special power,
Nor does it weaken me,
It does not label or have much meaning,
It's really not a thing.

My name is here like a shadow,
To give me a blanket of existence,
Shelter me,
Feed me,
Clothe me,

I do not complain.
Boo or hiss like the rain,
But smile like steel
To show the me inside the beast,
Proud I'll be of my name.

> — *Chandra Edwards*

The Precious Child

The Chinese name my grandmother gave me,
The name they thought would suit me,
The name I cherish till this day,
They named me "precious jade."

Down deep inside, inside of my heart,
The name seems so significant, a work of art,
When I say it, it has a special ring,
It gives me the feeling of being a king.

> — *Jennifer Lee*

This exploration of the meaning and family importance of names is particularly appropriate in second-language classes. A high school freshman from Iran wrote this poem about her name, Marjan-Miri, which means "coral" in Farsi.

Marjan, fluent in Farsi and German and quite capable in English, translated her poem for the class.

A Poem for My Name

My life full of wave of ocean.
Within beautiful colored fishes
carried by excitement of nature.
In the deep it's ruled by silence
and the whole creatures
having an amazing rest.
I continue living
with the pretty color red,
various branches like bright fired bushes.
By the time my life comes to the end
turning to a stone
I become for fashion, decoration
with expensive looks,
A passion was with this name
inside of my mother
so, she called me a coral.
In my country is MARJAN.
Now I still love this name
support it
and continue to pass it in my future
in remembering my mother.

Mother, I love you.

> — *Marjan-Miri Ghanizadeh*

5. LOVE POEMS

One of the considerations in writing about relationships is a long tradition of love poems. Look back at "Oranges," by Gary Soto, "Sonnet 116," by William Shakespeare, and "somewhere i have never travelled," by E.E. Cummings, under Poems for Discussion. To learn to write fresh and original love poems, we must read the old masters as well as the contemporary poets. The sonnets of Shakespeare surprise us even to this day, and the love poems by John Donne express the abstract emotions of love in images of science and technology. In the following translation of a sonnet by Dante, written about 1300, the poet uses very colloquial language to describe a daydream, a kind of proposal for an adventure in words we might easily use today.

Sonnet

Guido, I wish that you and Lapo and I
Were carried off by magic
And put in a boat which every time there was wind
Would sail on the ocean exactly where we wanted.

In this way storms and other dangerous weather
Wouldn't be able to harm us—
And I wish that, since we all were of one mind,
We would want more and more to be together

And I wish that Vanna and Lagia too
And the girl whose name on the list is number
   thirty
Were put in the boat by the magician too

And that we all did nothing but talk about love
And I wish that they were just as glad to be there
As I believe the three of us would be.

> — *Dante Alighieri*
> *translated by Kenneth Koch*

Elizabeth Barrett Browning's sonnet "How Do I Love Thee?" is one of the most beloved poems in the English language. This poem uses form of address, hyperbole, and elevated language, yet communicates a sincere expression of love.

How Do I Love Thee?

How do I love thee? Let me count the ways.
I love thee to the depth and breadth and height
My soul can reach, when feeling out of sight
For the ends of Being and ideal Grace.
I love thee to the level of everyday's
Most quiet need, by sun and candle-light.
I love thee freely, as men strive for Right;
I love thee purely, as they turn from Praise.
I love thee with the passion put to use
In my old griefs, and with my childhood's faith.
I love thee with a love I seemed to lose
With my lost saints,—I love thee with the breath,
Smiles, tears, of all my life!—and, if God choose,
I shall but love thee better after death.

> — *Elizabeth Barrett Browning*

In Gwendolyn Brooks's poem "To Be in Love," the "you" could mean the reader or refer to the writer herself. There is a blurring of the senses, of identity even, when two people love intensely. The poem refers to the game of emotions lovers play when they are being demure. The pleasure in words reflects the tangible delight between the lovers in the poem.

To Be in Love

To be in love
Is to touch things with a lighter hand.

In yourself you stretch, you are well.

You look at things
Through his eyes.
     A Cardinal is red.
     A sky is blue.
Suddenly you know he knows too.
He is not there but
You know you are tasting together
The winter, or light spring weather.

His hand to take your hand is overmuch.
Too much to bear.

You cannot look in his eyes
Because your pulse must not say
What must not be said.

When he
Shuts a door—
Is not there—
Your arms are water.

And you are free
With a ghastly freedom.

You are the beautiful half
Of a golden hurt.
You remember and covet his mouth,
To touch, to whisper on.

Oh when to declare
Is certain Death!

Oh when to apprize
Is to mesmerize,
To see fall down, the Column of Gold
Into the commonest ash.

— *Gwendolyn Brooks*

Often love poems are really about loss and sorrow. In this poem "Song," by Adrienne Rich, the writer explores the terrain of both personal and universal loneliness. Although abstract feeling introduces each stanza, simile and concrete images take over immediately to build a sense that strength grows out of the loneliness. In the last line, the poet has rebuilt a center able to love once again.

Song

You're wondering if I'm lonely:
OK then, yes, I'm lonely
as a plane rides lonely and level
on its radio beam, aiming across the Rockies
for the blue-strung aisles
of an airfield on the ocean

You want to ask, am I lonely?
Well, of course, lonely
as a woman driving across country
day after day, leaving behind
mile after mile
little towns she might have stopped
and lived and died in, lonely

If I'm lonely
it must be the loneliness

of waking first, of breathing
dawn's first cold breath on the city
of being awake
in a house wrapped in sleep
If I'm lonely
it's with the rowboat ice-fast on the shore
in the last red light of the year
that knows what it is, that knows it's neither
ice nor mud nor winter light
but wood, with a gift for burning.

— *Adrienne Rich*

In Federico García Lorca's poem "Variación," all three images use the senses and metaphor, but never mention love. The images are symbols of love. Even if you don't understand Spanish, read the Spanish version aloud, to hear the music of that language and how prevalent rhyming sounds are in Spanish.

Variación

El remanso del aire
bajo la rama del eco.

El remanso del agua
bajo franda de luceros.

El remanso de tu boca
bajo espesura de besos.

— *Federico García Lorca*

Variation

The still waters of the air
under the bough of the echo.

The still waters of the water
under a frond of stars.

The still waters of your mouth
under a thicket of kisses.

— *Federico García Lorca*

Langston Hughes uses repetition at the beginning of lines to set up a rhythm and momentum in this poem "Juke Box Love Song." It is a conjecture, a fantasy, a poem that addresses the girl he loves in language that reflects its urban setting.

Juke Box Love Song

I could take the Harlem night
and wrap around you,
Take the neon lights and make a crown,
Take the Lenox Avenue busses,
Taxis, subways,
And for your love song tone their rumble down.
Take Harlem's heartbeat,
Make a drumbeat,
Put it on a record, let it whirl,
and while we listen to it play,
Dance with you till day—
Dance with you, my sweet brown Harlem girl.

— *Langston Hughes*

Poetry Exercise #5

If you like, try a love poem that conveys a feeling of passion, respect, or loss. You might recall a first experience of being in a new relationship. Look back at "Oranges," by Gary Soto, in this chapter under Poems for Discussion. Try to stay away from abstract feeling, sentimentality, and cliché.

Student Examples

This poem by an eighth-grader was written as an exercise about oxymorons, but resulted in a passionate, unique statement about love.

Winter Autumn Eloquence

She is the most beautiful
She is the warmest, and most caring
She is the thing inside me,
that makes me want to run through the night
screaming hateful things at everyone
and everything
She is the most frightening
She is as cold as winter ice.
She cares for no one.
She is the thing inside me
that makes me sing and yell
and play wonderful music,
She is my best friend
She is my worst enemy
She makes me smile
She makes me cry, so that the tears
form a huge blue-green ocean
full of terrible and wonderful feelings.
I worship her house
I spit on her grave
I think of only her
I dance alone.
She thinks I am trash
She likes my style
She hates my wonderful music
with a passion
that forms a red-violet intensity
full of awfulness and jubilation.
She hates me
I hate her
I hate who she is
I hate what she is
Hate the things she does
I hate her sense of power
I hate the nights I spend
dreaming of her.
She hates me.
She hates who I am.
She hates what I am.
She hates the things I do.
She hates my sense of wealth.
She hates the nights she stays awake
thinking of reasons to hate me.
She is the thing inside me
that makes me write on the walls
and not trust, and hurt, and destroy.
She is the most wretched, the most merciful,
she is the most hungry, she is famine.
She is love, and right now, she is who
I live for.

— *Eddy Hogan*

Veux

(*a sonnet*)

Oh, how love takes me far the world and
'round!
O'er sweeping, rolling, dipping, gusting winds
And resting soon upon the emerald ground
When musical elation I will bring.
Through silken spires glinting in the sun;
Fiery, shining, burning, sweetly dizzy;
Buzzing with excitement, joy and fun,
And insides to and fro bubbly fizzy.
Now turning, spinning, flying 'bove the clouds,
I'm soaring wildly, diving, crazily free
Invincible, rambunctious, bold and loud,
Everything for one miraculous he.
Yes, leaping, warmth, fun and security;
Utter obsession—that is love to me.

—*Lillie S. Marshall*

A Secret Untold

The way he says little words
brings a smile to my face.
The way his shirt just barely
touches his rippled chest.
The way he laughs with that
tiny chuckle,
his glistening eyes,
his velvet lips,
his baby soft skin,
his walk,
his scent, that cologne that smells
fresh and clear on a hot and windy day.
The way it nips the top of my nose,
smells sweet but as tough as a black stallion.
The way he smoothed his talk with me was like
Romeo reciting his love for Juliet.
The way I feared I would fall in love with him
and everything about him.

— *Karina Rosado*

A Dream of Love

(*a sonnet*)

Come walk with me, we'll go into the forest,
Away from the city together we'll leave,
We shall find a clearing where we can rest
And hand in hand a dream of love we'll weave.

Up to the heavens together we'll go,
Through the leaves on sweet winds we will
soar,
We'll sail the skies, free cares below,
The earth below's now in your arms!

The night passes and the new day shall arise.
It's time to awake and break the seals of the
dream,
Awakening we set our eyes up to the skies;
We've come from the boundaries of the world
    of dreams.

For some they have nightmares of the death
above.
For those like us, we dream of the world of love.

— *Derek de Souza*

Como Yo Te Quiero?

Te dire de que formas?
Te quiero como el aire que se respira en el
campo.
Te quiero como las flores del jardín del Eden.
Te quiero como el agua cristalina
Te quiero como la luz del sol.
Te quiero como el amor que yo doy a Dios.
Te quiero como las alegría de los niños.
Te quiero como la Virgen Maria quiere a
su hijo Jesús.

— *Wanda Reynoso*

How Do I Love You?

Shall I tell you in what ways?
I love you like the air that you breathe
in the countryside.
I love you like the flowers
of the garden of Eden.
I love you like the crystalline water.
I love you like the light of the sun.
I love you like the love I give to God.
I love you like the joy of children.
I love you like the way the Virgin Mary
loves her son, Jesus.

— *Wanda Reynoso*
translated by Josefina Bosch

Ode to Love

Love
You are what holds people together
like a big piece of a puzzle.
Without you there is nothing.
Full of touching, hugging, kissing,
full of life, passion, and light.

You make me see what I've been missing.
Now I'm in the light,
No longer a shadow,
No longer depressed,
You make life easier
like a conclusion of a war.

— *Michelle Andrickson*

6. FINDING VOICE IN A NEW LANGUAGE

Even when second-language learners and bilingual students are given the choice of writing in their first languages, they are often eager to write in English, and these poems are often extremely risky and poignant. Why are students new to English so willing to write poetry in English and so successful in using their limited new vocabularies? Here are several possible reasons.

1. Poetry is an acceptable place to record issues and emotions, nonacademic thinking, the flood of feeling from home life and community, changes, separations, loneliness, freedom, exclusion, and identity issues.

2. Poetry has more flexibility in grammar usage, sometimes using sentence fragments, a word, or a phrase to deliver its message. A poem doesn't require the development of a whole paragraph of thought with a logical sequence: a beginning, middle, and an end. A poem doesn't have to sustain plot, character, narrative, and dialogue for many pages as a story does. The fact that a poem can be forceful and brief makes it more accessible to students eager to be heard and understood by classmates and friends.

3. Individual words carry considerable weight in poems. Students new to English often choose words carefully, looking up meanings of words, even asking about their connotations. They give more consideration to word sound and meaning than most native English speakers. Sometimes their slightly inappropriate use of a word or word-form or a pairing of two words not usually heard together gives the poem a freshness and surprise.

4. Many of these students come from cultures where poetry is read and heard as a matter of course at home or in school or as lyrics to songs. In many countries it is common to set poems to music, which moves them into the mainstream culture through radio and television. This happens frequently in Latin America, especially with Nueva Canción, as well as in Russia. In Israel the word for poem is the same as the word for song: *shir*. Many Hebrew poems enjoy widespread popularity through music and media exposure. Children from these and many other cultures are close to the cadences and rhythms of poetry.

Student Examples

My Grandmother's Hands

These are very old and rough hands.
There are a lot of veins in these hands.
But I love these hands because
these are my grandmother's hands.

I remember a long time ago
I was baby girl.

Every time I tumbled, these hands held
me, cleaned my pants.
Every time I was hungry, these hands
made cookies for me.
Every time I was cold, these hands
made a pretty coat for me.
Every time I wanted to go to sleep, these hands
put me in my bed.

These hands taught me what things are
good and what I can do.
I love these hands. I remember these
hands always.

— *Hui Xie*

Maki, an eighth-grader who had come from Japan a few years earlier, had said very little in seventh grade. Under the guidance of her teacher Phyllis Kutt, Maki began writing poems in eighth grade. This poem is a testament to what might stay buried in the heart of a child if no form were provided for its release.

Tomorrow Will Be Sunny

When I was 8 in the winter
The snow pile up in the city
My hands were numb

In the morning no one came to my house
Candlelight
Everybody loves Christmas

In my house my mother were waiting for me
Coughing and coughing
My mother were waiting for me

When I was young
There was love and shine
My family always smile

There was huge earthquake
And the Bank broke
Land, family, chair, also chopsticks were broke

My father said our money are all gone . . .
We didn't have any money and had family

If I had money for my father
If I had medicine for my mother
What was happiness
What was happiness
What was happiness
Grandpa and I dream together

It was snowing

— Maki

Chapter 6

Social and Global Issues

Introduction

Making Peace

A voice from the dark called out,
    "The poets must give us
imagination of peace, to oust the intense,
    familiar
imagination of disaster.   Peace is not merely
the absence of war."
               But peace, like a poem,
is not there ahead of itself,
can't be imagined before it is made,
can't be known except
in the words of its making.
grammar of justice,
syntax of mutual aid.
              A feeling towards
it,
dimly sensing a rhythm, is all we have
until we begin to utter its metaphors.
              A line of peace might
appear
if we restructure the sentence our lives are
    speaking:
shift from affirming profit and power,
question our needs, allow long pauses.
A cadence of peace might balance its weight
on a different fulcrum.
              Peace, a presence,
an energy field more intense than war,
might pulse then
stanza by stanza into the world,
each act
a word, each word
a vibration of light, facets
of the forming crystal.

              — *Denise Levertov*

Poems concerned with social and global issues have always been an important, moving force in the world. Many poems of protest have been written under adverse conditions and have expressed ideas that threatened the status quo. In some extreme cases, poems of protest have been expressed at the risk to the poet's life. A number of Latin American poets living under dictatorships have been forced into exile or have "disappeared."

Poets, like artists from all disciplines, have taken stances against war, greed, abuse of power, discrimination, oppression, and injustice. Because poems of protest express strong opinions and draw on such abstract ideas, they are the most difficult to write. Often, poets will use a flat tone in their poems to express their outrage through understatement. Symbols and metaphors provide another way of giving abstract feelings some roots in the experiential world. The use of juxtaposed points of view and of irony, even black humor, can be powerful tools to help craft the raw material of the poem of protest. Poetry and certain song lyrics have raised society's awareness of issues that needed immediate attention.

Poems for Discussion

OF WOMEN

1. Ain't I a Woman?

(*adapted from a speech*)
That man over there say
    a woman needs to be helped into carriages
and lifted over ditches
    and to have the best place everywhere.
Nobody ever helped me into carriages
    or over mud puddles
        or gives me a best place . . .
And ain't I a woman?
    Look at me
Look at my arm!
    I have plowed and planted
and gathered into barns
    and no man could head me . . .
And ain't I a woman?
    I could work as much
and eat as much as a man—
    when I could get to it—
and bear the lash as well
    and ain't I a woman?
I have born 13 children
    and seen most all sold into slavery
and when I cried out a mother's grief
    none but Jesus heard me . . .

and ain't I a woman?
     that little man in black there say
a woman can't have as much rights as a man
     cause Christ wasn't a woman
Where did your Christ come from?
     From God and a woman!
Man had nothing to do with him!
     If the first woman God ever made
was strong enough to turn the world
     upsidedown, all alone
together women ought to be able to turn it
     rightside up again.

— *Sojourner Truth*

2. My Mama Moved Among the Days

My Mama moved among the days
like a dreamwalker in a field;
seemed like what she touched was hers
seemed like what touched her couldn't hold,
she got us almost through the high grass
then seemed like she turned around and ran
right back in
right back on in

— *Lucille Clifton*

Of Justice at Home

3. Nice Day for a Lynching

The bloodhounds look like sad old judges
In a strange court. They point their noses
At the Negro jerking in the tight noose;
His feet spread crow-like above these
Honorable men who laugh as he chokes.

I don't know this black man.
I don't know these white men.

But I know that one of my hands
Is black, and one white. I know that
One part of me is being strangled,
While another part horribly laughs.

Until it changes,
I shall be forever killing; and be killed.

— *Kenneth Patchen*

4. To Make a Poem in Prison

It is hard
To make a poem in prison
The air lends itself not
to the singer.
The seasons creep by unseen
And spark no fresh fires.
Soft words are rare, and drunk drunk
against the clang of keys;
Wide eyes stare fat zeroes
And plead only for pity.

But pity is not for the poet;
Yet poems must be primed.
Here is not even sadness for singing,
Not even a beautiful rage rage,
No birds are winging. The air
Is empty of laughter. And love?
Why, love has flown,
Love has gone to glitten.

— *Etheridge Knight*

5. The Surrender Speech of Chief Joseph

I am tired of fighting.
Our chiefs are killed.
Looking Glass is dead.
Toohulhulsote is dead.
The old men are all dead.
It is the young men who say no and yes.
He who led the young men is dead.
It is cold and we have no blankets.
The little children are freezing to death.
My people, some of them, have run away
to the hills and have no blankets, no food.
No one knows where they are—
perhaps they are freezing to death.
I want to have time to look for my children
and see how many of them I can find.
Maybe I shall find them among the dead.
Hear me, my chiefs, I am tired.
My heart is sad and sick.
From where the sun now stands.
I will fight no more forever.

— *Chief of the Nez Percé tribe*

6. Looking For Indians

My head filled with tv images
of cowboys, warbonnets and renegades,
I ask my father
what kind of Indian are we, anyway.
I want to hear Cheyenne, Apache, Sioux,
words I know from television
but he says instead
Abenaki. I think he says Abernathy
like the man in the comic strip
and I know that's not Indian.

I follow behind him
in the garden
trying to step in his exact footprints,
stretching my stride to his.
His back is brown in the sun
and sweaty. My skin is brown
too, today, deep in midsummer,
but never as brown as his.

I follow behind him like this
from May to September
dropping seeds in the ground,
watering the tender shoots
tasting the first tomatoes,
plunging my arm, as he does,
deep into the mounded earth
beneath the purple-flowered plants
to feel for potatoes
big enough to eat.

I sit inside the bean teepee
and pick the smallest ones
to munch on. He tests
the corn for ripeness
with a fingernail, its dried silk
the color of my mother's hair.
We watch the winter squash grow hips.

This is what we do together
in summer, besides the fishing
that fills our plates unfailingly
when money is short.

One night
my father brings in a book.
See, he says, Abenaki,
and shows me the map
here and here and here
he says, all this

is Abenaki country.
I remember asking him
what did they do
these grandparents
and my disappointment
when he said no buffalo
roamed the thick new england forest
they hunted deer in winter
sometimes moose, but mostly
they were farmers
and fishermen.

I didn't want to talk about it.
Each night my father
came home from the factory
to plant and gather,
to cast the line out
over the dark evening pond,
with me, walking behind him,
looking for Indians.

— *Cheryl Savageau*

7. Frederick Douglass

When it is finally ours, this freedom, this liberty,
    this beautiful
and terrible thing, needful to man as air,
usable as earth; when it belongs at last to all,
when it is truly instinct, brain matter, diastole, systole,
reflect action; when it is finally won; when it is more
than the gaudy mumbo jumbo of politicians:
this man, this Douglass, this former slave, this Negro
beaten to his knees, exiled, visioning a world
where none is lonely, none hunted, alien,
this man, superb in love and logic, this man
shall be remembered. Oh, not with statues' rhetoric,
not with legends and poems and wreaths of bronze alone,
but with the lives grown out of his life, the lives
fleshing his dream of the beautiful needful thing.

— *Robert Hayden*

OF JUSTICE ABROAD

8. For Chile, 1977

It was a land where the winged mind
could alight.
Andean silver dazzling the Southern Cross;
the long shore of gold beaten by the Pacific
into translucency, vanishing
into Antarctica—

                  yes, these:
          but not for these
our minds flew there,

but because they knew
the poor were singing there
and the homeless
were building there
and the down trodden
were dancing.

How brief it was, that time
when Chile showed us how to rejoice!
How soon the executioners
arrived, making victims
of those who were not born to be victims.

The throats of singers
were punched into silence,
hands of builders
crushed,
dancers herded
into the pens.
                How few
all over the earth,
from pole to pole, are the lands
where our minds can perch and be glad,
clapping their wings, a phoenix flock!

From Chile now
they fly affrighted, evil smoke
rises from forest and city,
hopes are scorched.

When will the cheerful hammers sound again?
When will the wretched begin to dance again?
When will guitars again
give forth at the resurrected touch
or broken fingers
a song of revolution reborn?

                — *Denise Levertov*

9. Song for Soweto

At the throat of Soweto
a devil language falls
slashing
claw syllables to shred and leave
raw
the tongue of the young
girl
learning to sing
her own name
Where she would say
              water
They would teach her to cry
                blood
Where she would save
             grass
They would teach her to crave
                crawling into the
                    grave
Where she would praise
              father
They would teach her to pray
                somebody please
                do not take him
                away
Where she would kiss with her mouth
                my homeland
They would teach her to swallow
                this dust
But words live in the spirit of her face and that
sound will no longer yield to imperial erase
Where they would draw
             blood
She will drink
        water
Where they would deepen
             the grave
She will conjure up
        grass
Where they would take
             father and family away
She will stand
            under the sun/she will stay
Where they would teach her to swallow
                this dust
She will kiss with her mouth
             my homeland
and stay
with the song of Soweto
stay
with the song of Soweto

                — *June Jordan*

10. Dear Anne Frank

(*excerpts*)

I.

Comenzaron a prohibirte las bicicletas
a no salir pasadas las ocho,
a sólo comprar en ciertos almacenes
para judiós,
a sólo transitar por ciertas avenidas
a llevar una estrella dorada entre los brazos abier-
tos,
floridos.
Tus calles se poblaron de sedientos y
miedosos.
Tus pies dejaron de transitar por el aliento
del pasto
y sin embargo,
te gustaba la vida,
las mariposas,
las madrugadas de los que viajan
sin dirección precisa
con la estrella de David iluminándolos.

II.

Ana Frank,
brillosa y pequeña,
desvalida y valiente,
caminando con tu estrella dorada,
con la tristeza de los que preguntan
¿Por qué tú Ana Frank,
tatuada con los pesares de la historia?
¿Por qué no llevabas un girasol
en tus brazos
en vez de una
estrella sajada?

— *Marjorie Agosín*

I.

It began with the banning of your bicycles,
banning you from going out after eight at night,
restricting you to only buying goods in certain
shops for Jews,
to only walking down certain avenues
with a gold star between your open, blossoming
arms.
Your streets were filled with the thirsty and
fear-stricken.

Your feet quit crossing through windswept
pastures,
and yet
you loved life,
the butterflies,
dawns filled with all those wandering
in no particular direction,
the Star of David illuminating them.

II.

Anne Frank,
aglow and small,
destitute and brave,
walking with your gold star,
with the sadness of those who ask:
Why were you, Anne Frank,
tattooed with history's awful afflictions?
Why weren't you carrying a sunflower
against your breast
instead of a
lacerating star?

— *Marjorie Agosín*

OF WAR AND PEACE

11. The Man He Killed

"Had he and I but met
    By some old ancient inn,
We should have sat us down to wet
    Right many a nipperkin!

"But ranged as infantry,
    And staring face to face,
I shot at him as he at me,
    And killed him in his place.

"I shot him dead because—
    Because he was my foe,
Just so: my foe of course he was;
    that's clear enough; although

"He thought he'd list, perhaps,
    off-hand-like — just as I —
Was out of work — had sold his traps—
    No other reason why.

"Yes; quaint and curious war is!
    You shoot a fellow down
You'd treat, if met where any bar is,
    Or help to half-a-crown.

— *Thomas Hardy*

12. Facing It

My black face fades,
hiding inside the black granite.
I said I wouldn't,
dammit: No tears.
I'm stone. I'm flesh.
My clouded reflection eyes me
like a bird of prey, the profile of night
slanted against morning. I turn
this way—the stone lets me go.
I turn that way—I'm inside
the Vietnam Veterans Memorial
again, depending on the light
to make a difference.
I go down the 58,022 names,
half-expecting to find
my own in letters like smoke.
I touch the name Andrew Johnson;
I see the booby trap's white flash.
Names shimmer on a woman's blouse
but when she walks away
the names stay on the wall.
Brushstrokes flash, a red bird's
wings cutting across my stare.
The sky. A plane in the sky.
A white vet's image floats
closer to me, then his pale eyes
look through mine. I'm a window.
He's lost his right arm
inside the stone. In the black mirror
a woman's trying to erase names:
No, she's brushing a boy's hair.

                       — *Yusef Komunyakaa*

13. Sneaker Still-Life

A single solitary sneaker
lying amongst debris on dirt ground
next to a random mound of quiet rubble.
A still-life of a small town square
in a far away land.

An empty sneaker, an empty square,
a market place no longer there
on a bright sunny May morning.
A still death of a small town

in a far away land.

Brand new almost, this still white sneaker,
(size two male, nine or ten years old),
to be placed on a pile, all colors and every size.
Children taken from their worlds,
blown out of their sneakers
in a far away land.

Still spectators to mind numbing horror.
Still voices to the crying of children.
Still witnesses to a senseless century.
Still-life of a sneaker,
still warm in a far away land.

                       — *Fredric Lown*

14. So Long, Mom

(*a song for World War III*)

So long, Mom,
I'm off to drop the bomb,
So don't wait up for me,
But while you swelter
Down there in your shelter,
You can see me
On your T.V.

While we're attacking frontally,
Watch Brinkally and Huntally,
Describing contrapuntally
The cities we have lost.
No need for you to miss a minute of the
      agonizing holocaust.

Little Johnny Jones he was a U.S. pilot,
And no shrinking vi'let was he.
He was mighty proud when World War Three
      was declared,
He wasn't scared,
Nosiree!

And this is what he said on
His way to Armageddon:

So long, Mom,
I'm off to drop the bomb,
So don't wait up for me,
But though I may roam,
I'll come hack to my home,
Although it may be
A pile of debris.

Remember, Mommy,

I'm off to get a commie,
So send me a salami,
And try to smile somehow.
I'll look for you when the war is over,
An hour and a half from now.

— Tom Lehrer

Questions for Discussion and Analysis

1. Sojourner Truth uses at least three different concepts and levels of power to describe "woman." Identity these three perspectives of woman and show how they are sequenced in the poem. What is the significance of the repetition of the line, "And ain't I a woman?" How are "that little man in black" and "that man over there" connected? How does she use Christ to augment her concept of woman?

2. What is the tone of the poem "My Mama Moved Among the Days?" What does the "high grass" symbolize for the narrator and for the mother? There is an indefinite dreamlike quality to this whole poem. Besides the phrase "like a dreamwalker," how does Lucille Clifton create this blurry, yet vivid, picture of her mother. Is the narrator finding fault and passing judgment on her mother, or is she merely observing her from a distance?

3. How does Kenneth Patchen in a "Nice Day for a Lynching" describe the lynch mob? How does the tone of the first verse reflect the tone of the title? How does the narrator implicate himself and take responsibility for this horrible "injustice"? What does "it" refer to in the last verse? (*Note:* The "it" can be discussed in many contexts, from personal responsibility to the social implication of institutional racism.)

4. In Etheridge Knight's poem "To Make a Poem in Prison," what has happened to the poet's sources of material in the prison environment? Name each potential source

and how Knight conveys its absence. (*Note:* According to black oral tradition, the last word, "glitten," may have evolved from the word "glitter" when among slaves that code word meant to follow the stars, the glitter, or to run for freedom. Over time, it came to mean "leaving.") How does Knight create the prison environment through sound and the absence of sound? We think of the creation of art as needing freedom. What irony is evident in this poem, even in its title? Compare the line, "not even a beautiful rage rage" to the last line of Dylan Thomas's poem, "Do Not Go Gentle into That Good Night" in Chapter 5. How does this reference to Thomas's poem enlarge Knight's own poem?

5. In "The Surrender Speech of Chief Joseph," there is a powerful contrast between Chief Joseph's life force and his expression of death. How do these contrasting tones give power and credibility to his words? (*Note:* the life force can be heard in the present tense verbs I am, I can, I shall—while death is echoed through repetition at the ends of lines.)

6. Cheryl Savageau's poem "Looking For Indians" contains many themes including a child's quest for identity, parent-child bonding, and cultural ambivalence. Show how each of these themes is manifested in her poem. To grow up as a Native American watching cowboys and Indians on television must be a profoundly disturbing experience. How are other ethnic groups in our culture stereotyped?

7. Robert Hayden makes freedom and a great former slave/orator the subject of his passionate poem "Frederick Douglass." What images and comparisons make "freedom" necessary and physical? "What do we learn about Douglass's past and his vision? What legacy does he leave behind? How do we honor him, give substance to his vision? This poem is an irregular, mostly unrhymed sonnet. Why would the

poet choose a confining form and then break some of the rules associated with it?

8. (*Note:* In September of 1973 in Chile, a brief experiment in democratic socialism under the freely elected government of Salvador Allende Gossens came to a violent end. A bloody coup d'etat was carried out by General Pinochet, and the usurpers murdered President Allende and thousands of his followers. A military reign of terror followed this event and ended only after a Democratic election in 1989.)

   What "before" and "after" comparisons does Denise Levertov use in her poem "For Chile, 1977" to show the reader real events that occurred in Chile? What happened to the singers, the builders, and the dancers? In what ways is hope expressed in this poem? What universal themes emerge in this poem, and can you name any other place in the world where its events or message might be applicable?

9. (*Note:* Before reading "Song for Soweto," discuss the conflict in South Africa. Soweto is the largest urban black ghetto in Johannesburg, South Africa. It has been the scene of massive student rebellion against apartheid and unspeakable oppression during the 1970's and 1980's. Many young Soweto students went on strike in 1976 against the schools' policy of teaching in Afrikaans, the language of the settlers. Hundreds of students were killed in a confrontation with the police.)

   In June Jordan's poem "Song for Soweto," identify the "girl" and the "they." What does each person or force represent? Identify the two sections of the poem and their respective tones. What technique does Jordan use to give power to the girl?

10. In the first Marjorie Agosín excerpt about Anne Frank, how does the first line understate the cruelty of the Nazi regime? What technique does Agosín use involving the narrative voice that personalizes these poems for the reader? What does the Star of

David symbolize in each of these poems? How can it both illuminate and lacerate?

11. In "The Man He Killed," who are the "he" and "I" of the poem? How does Thomas Hardy compare these two characters? List similarities that exist between them. How does Hardy use understatement to evoke the horror of the war?

12. Show how Yusef Komunyakaa has created imagery that pulls the viewer of the Vietnam Veteran's Memorial into the wall. How are colors and light used as metaphors for both the war in Vietnam and the narrator's reactions to the war memorial? (Think of the spectrum of colors and light also as a metaphor for the spectrum of opinion about the war.) Which images do you feel are charged with emotion? Explain.

13. In "Sneaker Still-Life," Fredric Lown has personalized a somewhat remote event. How does the use of "sneaker" humanize this event and create immediacy and poignancy? Notice the different uses of the word "still." Show how "still" changes from a purely descriptive word to a politically charged word. Why does each verse repeat the same last phrase, "in a far away land"? Does this have the effect of bringing this event closer to the reader?

14. Why would poet-lyricist Tom Lehrer use humor to discuss nuclear holocaust in his song "So Long, Mom"? How do the irreverent lyrics help to raise the listener's awareness about issues related to the horrors of nuclear holocaust?

Bibliography of Additional Poems, Lyrics, and Books

Poems
"September 1, 1939," W. H. Auden
"Counting Small Boned Bodies," Robert Bly
"Martin Luther King Jr.," "The Blackstone Rangers: The Leader, Gang Girls," Gwendolyn Brooks

"We Wear the Mask," Paul Laurence Dunbar
"The Truth," Linda Hogan
"God to Hungry Child," "Park Bench,"
    Langston Hughes
"Ball Turret Gunner," Randall Jarrell
"After the Fall of Saigon" and "Boat People,"
    Yusef Komunyakaa
"What Were They Like," Denise Levertov
"The Children of Saigon" and "Christmas Bells,
    Saigon," Walter McDonald
"If We Must Die," Claude McKay
"The Dictators," Pablo Neruda
"Birmingham 1963," Raymond R. Patterson
"Barbie Doll," Marge Piercy
"Ballad of Birmingham," Dudley Randall
"Grass," Carl Sandburg
"At the Bomb Testing Site," William Stafford
"Vietnam Suite," Lamont Steptoe
"A Refusal to Mourn the Death, by Fire, of a
    Child in London," Dylan Thomas
"The Enemy's Eyes," Emma Lee Warrior
"Oh Captain, My Captain," "When Lilacs Last
    in the Dooryard Bloomed," Walt Whitman
"The Irish Airman Sees His Fate," William
    Butler Yeats

Lyrics

    Woody Guthrie, Pete Seeger/The Weavers
    Malvina Reynolds, Bob Dylan, Phil Ochs,
    Victor Jara, Paul Simon, Jackson Browne,
    Holly Near, Tracy Chapman, Sweet Honey
    in the Rock, U2, Arrested Development,
    TLC

Books

The Disappeared (also in Spanish), Marjorie
    Agosin,
Black Mesa Poems, Jimmy Santiago Baca
Prison Poems, Daniel Berrigan
The Light Around the Body, Robert Bly
To Disembark, Gwendolyn Brooks
Letters to Martha, Dennis Brutus
Next, Lucille Clifton
A Festering Sweetness, Robert Coles
The Country Between Us, Carolyn Forche
She Had Some Horses, Joy Harjo
In Evidence (poems from the words of World
    War II concentration camp liberators),
    Barbara Hyett

The Living Room, June Jordan
The Essential Etheridge Knight, Etheridge Knight
Dien, Cai Dau? and *Neon Vernacular*, Yusef
    Komunyakaa
Selected Poems, Primo Levi
Breaking Camp, Marge Piercy
Ceremony, Leslie Silko
I Never Saw Another Butterfly, Hana Volavkov'a,
    ed.
The Testing of Hannah Senesh, Ruth Whitman

Anthologies

The Poetry of Black America, Arnold Adoff, ed.
Atomic Ghost, Poets Respond to the Nuclear Age,
    John Bradley, ed.
Poems from the Turtle's Back (Contemporary
    Native American Poets), Joseph Bruchac, ed.
*Breaking Silence, An Anthology of Contemporary
    Asian American Poetry*, Joseph Bruchac, ed.
War Poetry, An Introductory Reader, Simon Feath-
    erstone, ed.
*Against Forgetting, Twentieth Century Poetry of
    Witness*, Carolyn Forche, ed.
In a Dark Time, Robert J. Lifton and Nicholas
    Humphrey, eds.
On Freedom's Side, Aaron Kramer, ed.
Holocaust Poetry, Hilda Schiff, ed.

Writing Exercises

1. WRITING A POEM OF SOCIAL CONSCIENCE

With your class, generate a list of social,
political, global, or moral issues or situations
they would like to see changed. These might
include questions about war and peace, issues
related to racism, sexism, ageism, poverty,
homelessness, human rights, environmental
issues, and general injustices suffered by
humanity.

How do poets transform their feelings of
anger and frustration about social issues into
poetry? Let's look at "Miss Rosie," by Lucille
Clifton.

Miss Rosie

When i watch you
wrapped up like garbage
sitting, surrounded by the smell
of too old potato peels
or
when i watch you
in your old man's shoes
with the little toe cut out
sitting, waiting for your mind
like next week's grocery
i say
when i watch you
you wet brown bag of a woman
who used to be the best looking gal in Georgia
used to be called the Georgia Rose
i stand up
through your destruction
i stand up

   — *Lucille Clifton*

What is this poem about? The poet doesn't try to deal with homelessness and poverty in the abstract. She focuses on one image, using the senses to create a portrait of a woman disintegrating. Her poem is meant to honor the homeless woman, to give humanity back to a person who has lost her identity. By capitalizing only the initial letters of Georgia Rose, she gives importance to a woman who has no more power in society. But the speaker will not let this woman's condition go unnoticed. She will be a witness, she will send a message through the poem. By limiting the poem to the image of one woman, the writer lets the reader make the connection to the larger issues of homelessness and poverty. The poet doesn't lecture, but moves the reader by presenting a real instance of a social condition.

In "Incident," Countee Cullen describes a real experience reflecting social relations. The prejudice the narrator encountered in Baltimore as an eight-year-old child resonates in his adult memory years later.

Incident

Once, riding in old Baltimore,
Heart-filled, head-filled with glee,
I saw a Baltimorean
Keep looking straight at me.

Now I was eight and very small,
And he was no whit bigger,
And so I smiled, but he poked out
His tongue, and called me, "Nigger."

I saw the whole of Baltimore
From May until December;
Of all the things that happened there
That's all that I remember.

   — *Countee Cullen*

Notice how through a simplicity of language Countee Cullen conveys complex feelings of racial prejudice and victimization. The memory carried from childhood of this singular incident does not strike the reader fully until the dramatic last line.

Poetry Exercise #1

Review the list of social/political issues you have created together and focus on one. Try to answer the following questions:

- What do you want the ultimate message of your poem to be?

- Who is the intended audience for your poem?

- What aspects of this issue would you like to change?

- Why do you feel strongly about this issue? What feelings does this issue evoke in you?

Once these questions are clarified, you can use some of the following techniques to craft your poem:

- Sketch in words a scene that portrays the human side of this issue. Look back at "Sneaker Still-Life," "Miss Rosie," and "Incident."

- Select sense images and similes or fragments of conversation that help make the subject of your poem less abstract.

- Consider ironic aspects of the scene that might add poignancy to your subject. (Look back at "The Man He Killed," by Thomas Hardy, where the narrator imagines sitting down to tea with a man who, in another context, is his enemy.)

Try to draft a poem focusing on *one* image or *one* event relating to the issue you have developed in your notes. Read your drafts in small groups, providing feedback on ways to strengthen the poem.

Student Examples

Old Newspapers

Old newspapers scattered along dirty sidewalks.
Crumpled soda cans lie in filthy corners.
Black chewing gum wedged into cement
    unnoticed.

Wilma Beth McCormack gracefully sits down
    on a
luxurious satin loveseat.
"James, some more tea please."
"Yes, your highness."
Wilma Beth McCormack bats her long
    lashes and
Smoothes out a wrinkle of her deep purple
    velvet gown.
Actually Wilma Beth McCormack is smoothing
out a wrinkle of her gray paper-thin shawl.

And actually "James" is the pigeon eating
a crumb out of her hand.

Oh, and in reality the satin loveseat is a
wet cardboard box that Wilma
calls home.

— Zoe

The Unlucky Ones

As we pile our shopping carts high with
    groceries
An old woman may be lying in the streets,
    starving.
As we climb into our warm, easy beds,
A young child wrapped in tattered rags lies
    sleeping in the cold outdoors.
But the lonely train stop is the only shelter for
    their frightened souls.
While we feast until we burst on
    Thanksgiving Day
They have nothing, no turkey, no stuffing.
"Do you have a dime for me?" an old man asks.
People on the streets just walk on past
    Although coins are jingling in their pockets.

— Nancy Elizabeth Lange

You, My Children

You bowing, you crying
You lying one day without knowing why
You struggling, while you watch others rest
You looking no longer with tears in your eyes
You my brother, dying, your face full
    of fear and suffering
So finally my children with all of this
    you stand up and shout!

                    — *Christopher Sands and Alexandra Pima*

War

What is a war?
An argument between
children?
A conflict between
friends?
But all of
these will quickly end.
What is a war?
A gun held tight in
someone's hand to
fire a bullet and
disturb the silence
What is a war?
Two shields and swords
or many against
each other
Swinging, slashing
cutting, trashing
or is it two men
in comfortable
recliners,
ready to
receive that signal?
and then
a mushroom
cloud bursts!
What is a war?
A game with cards
or a game with lives
Everyone killing to survive?
What is a war?

                    — *Natasha*

The Generation After

We have not known war—no—
To us the people on the field in battle
are a football team.
To us the surrounding cries
are high school fans,
not a low-flying bomber plane.

We have not known war—no—
To us a shriek at night
is the party across the street—
To us, a wailing screaming girl
has lost her boyfriend, not her family

We have not known war—no—
To us an authority at the door
is checking the burglar alarm,
To us a car in the dark
is a couple saying good-bye
after a date, not a family escaping.

We have not known war—no—
But when we do,
will there be a next generation?

                    — *Emily Michelson*

See Mattan's sonnet on war, "The Mother Speaks," in Chapter 7.

The following poems were written during studies of Facing History and Ourselves, a social studies curriculum exploring the duress of moral decision-making.

Walking to My Death

I walk,
Toward the death-grey building.
I know that I will die.
The doors open and I enter.
The doors clang behind me.
A young boy hands me a towel,
Looking at me with dead eyes.
Blank looks, gazing at me with guilt.
I forgive you—
They are making you do this.
I walk on.
A guard pulls my arm.

I look at him with hatred.
He looks at me with a grin of malice.
He shoves me into a small room.

I see a drop falling.

Now my ashes are on the ground,
My soul is up in Heaven.
Here I have a right,
A right to live freely forever.
My ashes are swept away.
You mix with other pure souls.
Now we live forever,
Never to be tortured again.

— *Kathleen Maeve Caulfield*

This next poem expresses the struggle of a teen-age student who is studying the Holocaust.

Don't Ask

I didn't ask to see
the heads of people,
bobbing on pencil necks,
eyes glazed over like,
a dead fish.

I didn't ask to see,
fields of gray,
barren and empty,
a graveyard full of
people gone away.
I didn't ask to see,
the camps of Nazis,
chambers dark and gray,
ominous and forbidden,
full of life all gone away.
I didn't ask to see
the pits dark and deep,
fires on the bottom,
burning away
people's calls and echoes.

My momma told me,
don't ask to see it,
it's too terrible,
for a child to see, so I don't ask,

But I see it anyway.

— *Aliza*

2. Extended Metaphor and Symbol

Is there a concrete symbol that might stand for an abstract issue? Write "Freedom" at the top of the board and ask your students for concrete objects that might stand for free-dom (the flag, the wind, a horse galloping, people gathered in a square, water flowing across rocks and beaches, a bird). What about "Confinement" (an animal trapped, a planet in orbit, a plant unable to reach out to light, a child in a playpen, a fly in a spider web)? Such symbols may be used as a meta-phor for an abstract idea. If the metaphor holds up throughout the whole poem, it is called an extended metaphor. Paul Laurence Dunbar uses the metaphor of a caged bird to represent one condition of human suffering.

Sympathy

I know what the caged bird feels, alas!
When the sun is bright on the upland slopes;
When the wind stirs soft through the springing grass
And the river flows like a stream of glass;
When the first bird sings and the first bud opens,
And the faint perfume from its chalice steals—
I know what the caged bird feels!

I know why the caged bird beats his wing
Till its blood is red on the cruel bars;
For he must fly back to his perch and cling
When he fain would be on the bough a-swing;
And a pain still throbs in the old, old scars
And they pulse again with a keener sting—
I know why he beats his wings!

I know why the caged bird sings, ah me,
When his wing is bruised and his bosom sore,—
When he beats his bars and would be free;
It is not a carol of joy or glee,
But a prayer that he sends from his heart's deep core,
But a plea, that upward to Heaven he flings
I know why the caged bird sings.

— *Paul Laurence Dunbar*

The denial of freedom causing pain, sorrow, humiliation, and rage are all expressed in "Sympathy." The symbol of the caged bird becomes an extended metaphor in that it represents all forms of human enslavement and imprisonment. Now look back at Maya Angelou's poem "Caged Bird" in Chapter 2, page 26, in the section Animals as Symbols. (Angelou borrows the metaphor from Dunbar's poem "Sympathy." Writers often honor their mentors and models by referring to their images and metaphors.) When an extended metaphor is successful, the poem has two levels of meaning. In "Caged Bird," the symbol of the free versus the caged bird creates a visual image of these two different birds' lives. Yet, the more universal meaning, contrasting the lives of enslaved and free people, works through the complete poem.

In "A Little Boy (and) a Giant Eclipse" by Fredric Lown, the narrator's son is watching a real eclipse. Using military imagery, the boy becomes a soldier protecting life from being eclipsed by war. Through extended metaphor, the author uses the eclipse to symbolize the ravages of the twentieth century.

A Little Boy (and) a Giant Eclipse

(for Zac, age 12)

Bundled under blue army blankets,
alone in the dimming dusk of winter,
lying on a cold lounger looking
through binoculars focused upward,
my little sentry at his outpost and
full of moon eyes aglow with wonder.

Are there enemy planes on your horizon?
Will you be spared the jungles and deserts?
When will you know of wargreed and bloodlust?

Our century was eclipsed by war rage,
ravaged by ignorance, hatred and profit,
betrayed by all who focused downwards.

Hold to your vision, my little sentry and
be gentle at our fragile outpost.

— *Fredric Lown*

In "Sympathy" and in "A Little Boy (and) a Giant Eclipse," both poets have focused on single images to symbolize universal issues of injustice and war.

Poetry Exercise #2

Think about an image (such as a little boy under an army blanket) or a symbol (such as a caged bird) and develop it to represent a social or global issue. Try to sustain this metaphor throughout the whole poem.

Student Examples

The Piano

When I sit down at my piano,
My fingers ready to play,
I treat the black and white keys
As equals every day.

But some folks play the white,
much more than they play the black,
Because some folks say the white,
Play much better than the black.

I've heard folks,
Who say it's wrong,
To play unequally,
But they're playing a lost song.

I say we've come a long way,
Since my grampa played,
He used to play only white.
See how much progress we've made.

— *Sam Kolb*

The Confused Zebra

The confused Zebra
Not knowing which way to go,
Its stripes confused it,
They mixed up its mind.
Should it go with its white stripes
or with its black?
It was accepted into both crowds.
Should it be dark like the night?
Should it be light like the day?
The confused Zebra
Not knowing which way to go.

— *Nicole*

3. WRITING SONG LYRICS AS AN EXPRESSION OF SOCIAL PROTEST

Return to the lyrics by Tom Lehrer, "So Long, Mom." Both in poetry and in song, satire is a very effective way to deliver a point of view about a disturbing or controversial subject. While the subject of nuclear threat is one that many people would rather avoid, Lehrer's satirical humor has made listeners laugh while reminding them about the more dour aspects of nuclear confrontation and the ludicrousness of war in the technological age. One of the devices that results in successful humor in song lyrics is clever rhyming. End rhymes that are multisyllabic have an unexpected delight or irony.

In contrast to Lehrer's lyrics is the song "Biko," written by Bernice Johnson Reagon of Sweet Honey in the Rock. This song, which invokes the South African leader Stephen Biko through constant repetition of his name, delivers a message of the spread of hatred from South Africa to America. It draws on the rhythms and images of the Bible and the phrasing of gospel music. Try to borrow the recording to hear how the phrases are sung.

Biko

Biko-Biko-Biko
here comes Stephen Biko
Walking down the waters
Hey-Hey whatcha gon do with Biko
Biko-Biko

Waters of fear and hatred
Waters of starving babies
Hey-Hey whatcha gon do with Biko
    Biko-Biko
Come all the way from Capetown
    to Wilmington, North Carolina
Hey-Hey whatcha gon do with Biko
    Biko-Biko

You can break one human body
I see ten thousand Biko's
Hey-Hey whatcha gon do with Biko
    Biko-Biko

*— Bernice Johnson Reagon
founder of Sweet Honey in the Rock*

There is a long history of American folk songs of protest, sung by eminent singer/songwriters such as Woody Guthrie, Pete Seeger, Malvina Reynolds, Peter, Paul and Mary, and Bob Dylan. The songs have dealt with Native American issues, women's right to vote, child labor, union organizing, civil rights, and war and peace. You might bring in old recordings of "This Land Is Your Land," "Blowin' in the Wind," "Deportee," "Last Night I Had the Strangest Dream," "Masters of War," and "Joe Hill." This last song, a ballad with lyrics written by Alfred Hayes and popularized by Pete Seeger, recounts the story of a famous union organizer in Utah in 1915. Joe Hill was accused of shooting a storekeeper, was convicted, and was executed. His trial and execution caused a national and international stir at the time. Many people believed he was framed for this murder because of his union activities.

Joe Hill

I dreamed I saw Joe Hill last night,
Alive as you and me;
Says I "But Joe, you're ten years dead."
"I never died," says he.

"In Salt Lake, Joe, by God," says I,
Him standing by my bed,
"They framed you on a murder charge."
Says Joe, "But I ain't dead."

"The copper bosses killed you, Joe.
They shot you, Joe," says I.
"Takes more than guns to kill a man,"
Says Joe, "I didn't die."

And standing there as big as life,
And smiling with his eyes,
Joe says, "What they forgot to kill
Went on to organize."

"Joe Hill ain't dead," he says to me,
"Joe Hill ain't never died.
Where workingmen are out on strike,
Joe Hill is at their side.

"From San Diego up to Maine,
In every mine and mill,
Where workers strike and organize,"
Says he, "You'll find Joe Hill."

I dreamed I saw Joe Hill last night,
Alive as you and me.
Says I, "But Joe, you're ten years dead."
"I never died," says he.

— *Alfred Hayes*

The ballad is the traditional form for narrating a story, and its simplicity allows the song to be passed along with ease.

Rap music has long been a vehicle for raising awareness about social issues and injustices. Rap adheres to a strict rhyme scheme and rhythm. The performers chant or half-sing the lyrics, which often are quite lengthy. KRS-One, Arrested Development, TLC, along with many others, have used the power of performance and the language of rap to encourage young people to avoid drugs and violence, to promote safe sex, and to raise their self-esteem.

Poetry/Songwriting Exercise #3

Focus on an issue that disturbs you. Consider the options of writing satire, spirituals, folk ballads, rap, blues, soul, or other contemporary forms of songs. You might borrow images, language style, rhythms, or even a melody from a particular song or genre of music. Write a draft of the lyrics first. Try to establish a consistent rhyme scheme and rhythm, if you so choose. Sing the words to yourself, and see how word choice and rhythm might be adjusted to follow your melody or beat more closely. Revise the lyrics several times until they mesh naturally with the music. You might sing your song to a friend, or tape it and play it for the class. You might choose to read your lyrics and ask a musical classmate to arrange some music for your song.

Student Examples

Blessed Be

(*written and sung in gospel style*)
Blessed be the changemakers
who try to change the ways
of this wicked world.
Blessed be to them who care enough
for the very best.
The changemakers of this world,
blessed be to them.
And blessed be to the people
who are trying to make a change.
Blessed be, blessed be
to the changemakers.

— *Tabitha Wilson*

Young Americans

All night, they were some young Americans
                                — *David Bowie*

Can ya hear me
I'm playin' away
can ya hear me
all night and all day

Go while you can
are you sleepin'
go while your mine
I'll be thinkin'

I'll tap the ivories
all of the night
I'll tap the ivories
the kids are all right

I'll sing a simple song
can't ya see
I'll sing a simple song
doe rae me

Can ya understand the music
wish I could
can ya understand the music
knock on wood

I'll tap my foot, I'll sing along
I'll play for you
I'll tap my foot, I'll sing along
a verse and a life for you

The blues is somethin' ya can't ignore
I hold it deep in my soul
The blues is somethin' I'll never ignore
as the snare makes a soft, soft roll

I'll sing for you every day
while the sweet blues take me away
I'll sing for you every day
while the sweet, sweet blues take me away

                                — *Zach Bloom*

Chapter 7

Form and Content: Sonnets, Villanelles, and Sestinas

Introduction

Over the course of history, poetic forms in America have evolved from or for songs, chants, religious ceremonies, and other structures of language primarily from Western cultures. The quatrain, four lines of verse, evolved from the ballad. The terza rima, three-line stanzas with interlocking rhymes, was invented by Dante for *The Divine Comedy* based on the idea of the Trinity. The sonnet, while developed in the 1200's, became a central fixture in poetic literature during the 1500's. Villanelles and sestinas were adapted from the verse-songs of the troubadours who wandered in Europe from the eleventh through the thirteenth centuries.

The English Romantic poets experimented with six- and eight-line stanzas with various rhyme schemes and meters. William Butler Yeats, in the early 1900's, moved away from his lyrical verses and used irregular rhymes and meters to reflect his themes of political upheaval.

In America before the turn of the century, Emily Dickinson borrowed the tight forms of the church hymn and used slant rhymes (rhymes that are not exact) in almost all of her poems. In contrast, Walt Whitman discarded all the rules with his long, effusive, unrhymed lines which sang the praises of both himself and his country. Almost single-handedly, Whitman broke away from the entire tradition of Western European poetic literature and began a new era of experimentation in poetic language. In the early 1900's, T.S. Eliot and Ezra Pound often combined the use of tight traditional forms with more narrative prose-like passages. Amy Lowell rooted her free verse poems in striking visual imagery. William Carlos Williams developed a diction based on image and direct speech. Robert Frost listened for the shapes and cadences of conversation and overlaid those patterns on the old forms and their variations. Marianne Moore sometimes created forms from lines of particular syllabic length.

Langston Hughes listened carefully to the musical forms of African-American culture and adapted the blues and jazz to his poems. E.E. Cummings often used traditional forms disguised with unconventional punctuation and syntax. The early beat poets rejected form as part of their political content. Contemporary Native American poets draw on the repetitive chant forms of their past. Since the 1960's when women writers and writers of color have had the opportunity to publish and be heard, every aspect of form and content has been challenged and reintegrated.

When new voices are heard, the language changes and its forms and literary traditions broaden and grow richer. Also, as in every aspect of culture, there are cycles of styles. Traditional forms were out of style from the fifties through the seventies and reemerged in published poems during the eighties and nineties.

Because of the changing nature of literary style and because our American literature now represents such a broad spectrum of voices, it is especially important for students to hear poems that represent each era and the styles and new forms that reflect our many cultures.

Harmony of Form and Content

When students learn to recognize forms and come to understand various experiments with poetic language in terms of shape, rhythm, and syntax, they will be able to take more pleasure in the poems they read and begin to see the connection between content (the subject matter) and the chosen form. The English lyric form, a metered, rhymed structure, seems natural and appropriate to sing the praises of nature. But the English lyric would be unsuitable for expressing the experience of the black American slave, whereas the blues form intensifies the meaning of such a poem. Walt Whitman's expansive lines seem to be the perfect form for his ebullient praise, while Emily Dickinson's concise hymns or riddles are better suited to her questions and introspections. Robert Frost's metered phrasing of New England speech patterns suits his poems about the harshness of the rural life, but would seem unnatural and forced if used with the political outcries of the California beat poets.

The merging of form and content is a difficult and intuitive process, one which comes with years of practicing the craft of writing poems and with extensive reading and studying of poetic literature. Nonetheless, students must select a form for their poetic expression. It is easiest for them to articulate their meaning and imagery while writing in a free verse style. In subsequent drafts, they may wish to experiment with line and stanza breaks. However, as they read and learn to recognize a variety of forms, they may wish to attempt a particular form. The first question should be, Is this content appropriate to the form? If the student selects the sonnet form, then the material must be focused, the images tight. If the student chooses the villanelle or terza rima, there should be something cyclical or insistent about the material to integrate with the repeating lines. Look back at "Do Not Go Gentle into That Good Night," by Dylan Thomas, under Poems for Discussion in Chapter 5. Both the inevitability of aging and death and the son's admonition to his father not to give up life without a fight are appropriate themes for the villanelle. In a sestina, the content should be broader, more explorative. By attempting to write in a form, young writers can experience the intellectual pleasure of molding their ideas and images into a formal structure. Through trial and error, they come to see what source material might be heightened and intensified by a particular form.

In general, high school students would benefit most from these exercises in form. However, some seventh- and eighth-graders will be ready to try one, and this chapter presents three possibilities: the sonnet from the European literary tradition, villanelles, and sestinas from troubadours of the Middle Ages.

Praise poems, discussed in Chapter 8, offer a contrasting style of writing, and a release from the constraints of classical forms.

The haiku, renga, senryu, and tanka are forms which we have inherited from various Asian cultures. They are brief forms, based on syllabics or on a certain kind of focus or image. The ghazal was developed in Persia. *The Handbook of Poetic Forms*, published by the Teachers and Writers Collaborative, contains a history and explanation of these forms and offers other options not described in this chapter.

High school and college-level texts that will supplement the teaching of form include *Western Wind*, by John Frederick Nims, and *Introduction to Poetry*, by X.J. Kennedy.

The Sonnet

Secondary school students, beginning with seventh-graders who have read and written poetry, may be ready for and attracted to more sophisticated techniques, including such forms as the sonnet, villanelle, and sestina. Students who have a proclivity for writing poetry are more receptive to the parallel craftsmanship required. Writing in these forms assumes a level of comfort with rhyme scheme and meter. While introducing examples of poems in various forms, direct your students to listen for patterns in stressed and unstressed syllables. Students might begin to identify various meters and to count out the number of beats in a line. (See glossary for the most common traditional meters.) Exercises that introduce students to the simple scanning of lines will help them identify particular forms and are essential if they wish to attempt to write in a form.

The sonnet is one of the most important of all poetic forms in Western literature. According to the *Handbook of Poetic Forms*, it is thought to have been invented around the year 1200 by the poet Giancomo da Lentino in Italy. Petrarch in the 1300's in Italy and Edmund Spenser and William Shakespeare in the 1500's refined the sonnet and raised it to a central form in the English language. Shakespeare wrote 154 sonnets, some of which are considered the greatest love poems in the English language. Traditionally, sonnets deal with love and unrequited love, aging, death, grief, joy, and the forces of the natural world. The most common form of the sonnet is a fourteen-line poem in two parts: an octave (eight lines) and a sestet (six lines), or three quatrains and a final couplet. The sonnet involves a certain way of thinking: An idea or thought is developed in the first eight lines, then brought to a conclusion in the final sestet or couplet. The brevity of the sonnet forces the poet to focus on one idea and to use concise, compressed language and imagery.

The sonnet is an exquisite form, a place where language, image, feeling, thought, rhythm, music, and rhyme fuse within the fourteen lines. Not only did the great classical poets refine this form, but most poets of the nineteenth and twentieth centuries, poets who write both in English and in other languages, have worked in this form at one time or another, following its traditions closely or experimenting with variations in some of its rules. Many of the poems by E.E. Cummings, which seem to push out the boundaries of syntax and grammar, are actually very formal sonnets, not evident at first from their appearance on the page. In her early work, Gwendolyn Brooks used the sonnet form for messages about the black experience, bridging the gap between inherited Western European forms and an exploration of new material. Pablo Neruda published *100 Love Sonnets*, available in Spanish and English. Stanley Kunitz wrote fifty love sonnets without rhyme.

To recognize the form gives deep pleasure to the reader. To feel comfort with the form as a writer provides an intense feeling of accomplishment. This chapter suggests ways to read, analyze, and help students write sonnets of their own.

Recognizing Sonnets and Their Variations

Students have probably encountered poems in quatrains, four-line stanzas that may be nonrhyming or have rhyme schemes such as ABCB, ABAB, or ABAA, as in the blues. Popular song lyrics are frequently written in this form, and you might ask students to bring in their favorite examples and identify the rhyme schemes. Lyrics can be used to discuss number

of beats in a line and where stresses fall. Refer to lyrics of songs by Bob Dylan, the Beatles, Joni Mitchell, Cole Porter, Tom Lehrer, Sting, Whitney Houston, and such blues artists as Huddy Ledbetter and Bessie Smith. (A further discussion of songwriting patterns can be found in Chapter 6.)

The traditional sonnet is comprised of 14 lines: an octave, sometimes divided into two quatrains; and a sestet, which may be divided into a quatrain and a couplet. It is written in the meter of iambic pentameter: One iamb is an unstressed syllable followed by a stressed syllable (-/) with five iambs to a line (-/-/-/-/-/). The Shakespearean sonnet follows this rhyme scheme: ABAB, CDCD, EFEF, GG. Petrarch, earlier in Italy, developed a more confining rhyme scheme: ABBA, ABBA, CDCDCD (or CDECDE or other possibilities for the final sestet), which is still a very popular form. Spenser, Wordsworth, Hopkins, and many other writers created variations on these structures. "Once by the Pacific," by Robert Frost, uses seven rhyming couplets instead of quatrains.

Poems for Discussion

1. Sonnet 36

Let me confess that we two must be twain,
Although our undivided loves are one;
So shall these blots that do with me remain,
Without thy help, by me be borne alone.
In our two loves there is but one respect,
Though in our lives a separable spite,
Which though it alter not love's sole effect,
Yet doth it steal sweet hours from love's delight.
I may not evermore acknowledge thee,
Lest my bewailed guilt should do thee shame;
Nor thou with public kindness honour me,
Unless thou take that honour from thy name:
   But do not so; I love thee in such sort,
   As, thou being mine, mine is thy good report.

— *William Shakespeare*

2. Romeo and Juliet

(*Act I, Scene V*)

Romeo
If I profane with my unworthiest hand
This holy shrine, the gentle fine is this;
My lips, two blushing pilgrims, ready stand
To smooth that rough touch with a tender kiss.

Juliet
Good pilgrim, you do wrong your hand too much,
which mannerly devotion shows in this;
For saints have hands that pilgrims' handdo touch,
And palm to palm is holy palmers' kiss.

Romeo
Have not saints lips, and holy palmers too?

Juliet
Ay, pilgrim, lips that they must use in prayer.

Romeo
O, then, dear saint, let lips do what hands do!
They pray; grant thou, lest faith turn to despair.

Juliet
Saints do not move, though grant for prayers' sake.

Romeo
Then move not while my prayer's effect I take
[*Kisses her.*]
Thus from my lips, by thine my sin is purged.

Juliet
Then have my lips the sin that they have took.

Romeo
Sin from my lips? O trespass sweetly urged!
Give me my sin again. [*Kisses her.*]

Juliet
You kiss by the book.

— *William Shakespeare*

3. How Do I Love Thee?

How do I love thee? Let me count the ways.
I love thee to the depth and breadth and height
My soul can reach, when feeling out of sight
For the ends of Being and ideal Grace.
I love thee to the level of everyday's
Most quiet need, by sun and candle-light.
I love thee freely, as men strive for Right;
I love thee purely, as they turn from Praise.
I love thee with the passion put to use
In my old griefs, and with my childhood's faith.
I love thee with a love I seemed to lose
With my lost saints,—I love thee with the breath,
Smiles, tears, of all my life!—and, if God choose,
I shall but love thee better after death.

— *Elizabeth Barrett Browning*

4. Once by the Pacific

The shattered water made a misty din.
Great waves looked over others coming in,
And thought of doing something to the shore
That water never did to land before.
The clouds were low and hairy in the skies,
Like locks blown forward in the gleam of eyes.
You could not tell, and yet it looked as if
The shore was lucky in being backed by cliff,
The cliff in being backed by continent;
I looked as if a night of dark intent
Was coming, and not only a night, an age.
Someone had better be prepared for rage.
There would be more than ocean-water broken
Before God's last *Put out the Light* was spoken.

— *Robert Frost*

5. Childhood

When I was a child I knew red miners
dressed raggedly and wearing carbide lamps.
I saw them come down red hills to their camps
dyed with red dust from old Ishkooda mines.
Night after night I met them on the roads,
or on the streets in town I caught their glance;
the swing of dinner buckets in their hands,
and grumbling undermining all their words.

I also lived in low cotton country
where moonlight hovered over ripe haystacks,
or stumps of trees, and croppers' rotting shacks
with famine, terror, flood, and plague near by;
where sentiment and hatred still held sway
and only bitter land was washed away.

— *Margaret Walker*

6. #24

"next to of course god America I
love you land of the pilgrims' and so forth oh
say can you see by the dawn's early my
country 'tis of centuries come and go
and are no more what of it we should worry
in every language even deafanddumb
thy sons acclaim your glorious name by gorry
by jingo by gee by gosh by gum
why talk of beauty what could be more beautiful than these heroic happy dead
who rushed like lions to the roaring slaughter
they did not stop to think they died instead
then shall the voice of liberty be mute?"

He spoke. And drank rapidly a glass of water

— *e.e. cummings*

7. The Pupil

Picture me, the shy pupil at the door,
One small, tight fist clutching the dread Czerny.
In those days time was harmony still, not money,
And I would spend the whole week practicing for
That moment on the threshold.

                         Then to take courage,
And enter, and pass among mysterious scents,
And sit there straight, and with a frail confidence
Assault the keyboard with a childish flourish!

Only to lose one's place, or forget the key,
And almost doubt the very metronome
(Outside, the traffic, the laborers going home),
But still to bear on across Chopin or Brahms,
Stupid and wild with love equally for the storms
Of C sharp minor and the calms of C.

— *Donald Justice*

8. Turnabout

The old dog used to herd me through the street
As if the leash were for my benefit,
And when our walk was over he would sit
A friendly jailer, zealous, at my feet.
My children would pretend that they felt fine
When I was anxious at some hurt of theirs

As if they were the parents, for the tears
At their predicaments were often mine.

And now against the whiteness of the sheet
My mother, white faced, comforts with the story
of Brahms, the boy, who couldn't sleep for worry
Until a chord achieved its harmony,
So down the stairs he crept to play the C.
She means her death will make a circle complete.

— *Linda Pastan*

9. Looking

You have not word for soldiers to enjoy
The feel of, as an apple, and the chew
With masculine satisfaction. Not "good-by!"
"Come back!" or "careful!" Look, and let him go.
"Good-by!" is brutal, and "come back!" the raw
Insistence of an idle desperation
Since could he favor he would favor now.
He will be "careful!" if he has permission.
Looking is better. At the dissolution
Grab greatly with the eye, crush in a steel
Of study—even that is vain. Expression.
The touch or look or work will little avail.
The brawniest will not beat back the storm
Nor the heaviest haul your little boy from harm.

— *Gwendolyn Brooks*

10. A Lovely Love

Let it be alleys. Let it be a hall
Whose janitor javelins epithet and thought
To cheapen hyacinth darkness that we sought
And played we found, rot, make the petals fall.
Let it be stairways, and a splintery box
Where you have thrown me, scraped me with
    your kiss,
Have honed me, have released me after this
Cavern kindness, smiled away our shocks.
That is the birthright of our lovely love
In swaddling clothes. Not like that Other one.
Not lit by any fondling star above.
Not found by any wise men, either. Run.
People are coming. They must not catch us here
Definitionless in this strict atmosphere.

— *Gwendolyn Brooks*

Questions for Discussion and Analysis

1. Review the rules of the traditional sonnet with regard to Shakespeare's "Sonnet 36." Mark the rhyme scheme on the poem at the end of each line, using a new letter from the alphabet for each new unrhymed word introduced: ("twain"=A), ("one"=B), ("remain"=A), etc. Can you read the first four lines in a normal voice, then exaggerate the meter? Scan the first four lines by indicating unstressed (˘) and stressed (/) syllables. The first line should look like this: ("Lĕt mé cŏnféss thăt wé twŏ múst bĕ twáin"). This sonnet is a perfect companion to the sonnet from Romeo and Juliet (#2 of the Discussion Poems). Both the play and this sonnet explore the theme of love that can't be acknowledged. Can you restate Shakespeare's meaning? Try it line by line. How does the final couplet change in attitude?

2. William Shakespeare's love sonnet in *Romeo and Juliet*, Act I, Scene V, is in dialogue form and indicates a moment of high drama and passion. These are the *first* words they say to each other. In your own words, describe how Romeo talks Juliet into kissing. Identify the rhyme scheme and meter. Where in this portion of dialogue does the sonnet end?

3. What is the rhyme scheme of Elizabeth Barrett Browning's sonnet "How Do I Love Thee?" How does the poet make the abstract idea of love more real? Who is addressed in the poem? Where does the poet begin to sum up her feelings?

4. In Robert Frost's "Once by the Pacific," how does his rhyme scheme differ from that of the traditional Shakespearean sonnet? On what imagery does the poem focus? What abstract idea does Frost move toward by the end? How is the sonnet related to the rhythms and motions of the sea?

5. What variations on a Petrarchan sonnet does Margaret Walker use in her poem "Childhood"? Think about the places she lived and the daily rituals of miners and sharecrop-

pers. How does the predictability of hardship relate to the formality of the sonnet? How has Margaret Walker broken away from the traditional material of sonnets?

6. In E.E. Cummings's sonnet #24, "next to of course god . . . ," how does the poet alter the sonnet form? What kind of diction does the poet use that seems to go against the traditional sonnet subject and language? Where does the poet begin to change the direction of the poem? What is the poet's message? Why would he choose the sonnet form for a satire?

7. In "The Pupil," by Donald Justice, what moment is the poet describing? How does the poem keep within the sonnet tradition while its shape breaks up on the page? Where does the poet use slant rhyme? Think about the ideas of harmony and resolution in music. What is the parallel with rhyme and meter in poetry? Notice how the piece of music and the poem resolve together.

8. In "Turnabout," by Linda Pastan, identify the rhyme scheme and how this sonnet varies from classical forms. What three situations has the poet set up to illustrate the turnabout? Where does the summation of the poem's ideas occur? How is this different from the traditional arrangement? Discuss how the subject matter is narrowed and compressed in order to be harmonious with the sonnet form. Look back at "The Pupil." Both poems use the idea of the resolving final C chord. What emotions are connected to this image in each poem? Why did Pastan use the final word "complete," which rhymes with the end word of the first line?

9. In Gwendolyn Brooks's sonnet "Looking," who is addressed? Who might be the speaker? How is this antiwar sentiment made familiar or personal to the reader? What kind of sonnet is this? How does the consistent use of slant rhyme throughout the poem reflect the poet's message?

10. In "A Lovely Love," by Gwendolyn Brooks, where are some of the places she

suggests desperate lovers might meet? What sounds, smells, and textures does she use to make these places real? The "love" itself is so new, it is in "swaddling clothes." Using that clue, "fondling star," and "wise men," who is "that Other one?" Where might "this strict atmosphere" be? While one birth is blessed, how is the birth of this "lovely love" viewed? How does the poet fuse two variations of the classical sonnet? How is the confinement of the sonnet related to the meaning of the poem?

Bibliography of Additional Poems and Books

The Sonnet, an Anthology, Robert M. Binder and Charles L. Squier, eds.

"To My Dear and Loving Husband," Ann Bradstreet

Blacks, Gwendolyn Brooks

Sonnets from the Portuguese, Elizabeth Barrett Browning

"Yet Do I Marvel," Countee Cullen

"i thank You God for most this amazing" and *100 Selected Poem,* E.E. Cummings

Collected Poem, Robert Frost

"Frederick Douglass" (see Poems for Discussion, Chapter 6), Robert Hayden

"Sonnet to a Negro in Harlem," Helene Johnson

50 Love Sonnets, Stanley Kunit

*Collected Sonnets*122, Edna St. Vincent Millay

100 Love Sonnets, Pablo Neruda

The Songs and Sonnets of William Shakespeare, William Shakespeare

"Substitution," Anne Spencer

"The World Is Too Much with Us," William Wordsworth

Writing Exercises

1. FIRST SONNET

Once students can recognize the form of a sonnet, discuss its rhythms and turning points, and feel comfortable with reading sonnets aloud, you might suggest they try writing one. For a first sonnet-writing exercise, you might suggest a topic that is common to most students in the class, yet is focused and emotional. Eighth-graders or twelfth-graders about to graduate from their school could be asked to use the form to reflect on their educational experience so far. The first eight or twelve lines might mention specific events or relationships from their past years in school. The final sestet or couplet could express their feelings of hope or anxiety for their future. While students might groan about being confined to this subject matter, the exercise demonstrates how a writer might organize thoughts consistent with the sonnet form.

Ask your students to generate a list of images, memories, and events from school that have had meaning for them over the past years. Invite each student to offer two or three ideas aloud. List the ideas on the board. Try writing one quatrain collaboratively on the board, drawing on the recorded images. Ask your students to write another quatrain during the class period. As they read aloud, your feedback will help them solidify the techniques. For homework, have your students select three significant images or ideas for their three quatrains. They should select a specific rhyme scheme and write one quatrain for each idea. Have students read their work aloud the next day and discuss ways to smooth out rhythms and keep language from sounding awkward and inverted. In contemporary poetry, value is placed on using language that is close to natural speech, not restructured in a forced way, in order to arrive at a desired rhyme. Students can consider half rhymes or slant rhymes when their rhyming words become too predictable or trite. These are rhymes where only the consonants or the vowels are repeated sounds, rather than both interior vowels and final consonants (for example, "pla<u>nt</u> / hu<u>nt</u>" or "pl<u>ant</u> / gr<u>and</u>").

Students should complete a first draft of a sonnet. They can use the form provided on the next page. Select several first drafts to be photocopied for discussion. Class comments will reveal where meaning is unclear, where images can be strengthened, where the form is collapsing, and where rhymes might be fresher.

Shakespearean Sonnet Form

Directions: Write a sonnet, using iambic pentameter, -/-/-/-/-/, or close to ten syllables.

_____ A

_____ B

_____ A

_____ B

_____ C

_____ D

_____ C

_____ D

_____ E

_____ F

_____ E

_____ F

_____ G

_____ G

Student Examples

In the following sonnet, Stacy used the first three quatrains to enumerate her experiences at Heath School. The final couplet sets her prior schooling against the uncertainties and excitement of her future. Throughout, her rhymes are unexpected and sophisticated. Her slant rhymes of "graduation" and "anticipation" are particularly skillful.

Heath School

So long ago when milk was just a dime
and since then so much more than price has
   changed,
These memories of Heath will fade with time,
as high school makes my whole life rearrange.

These halls we've roamed for more than half
   our years
from Kindergarten innocence of past,
to recent times of pressures, stress, and tears.
Not all relationships are meant to last.

Counting days until our graduation
instead of having fun while I was here,
I've wasted years on false anticipation,
and now the thought of high school brings me fear.

I'm trading in all Heath's security
For what's behind the curtain Number Three.

               — *Stacy Roalsen*

It All Began

It all began with crayons and paper,
Then the "Lorax" and the "Cat and the Hat,"
Now it's tons of homework and fun later,
Now it's a softball and a baseball bat.

Before it was boys chase girls and cooties,
Now it's romance and love at first sight.
Before it was fun, silly cartoonies,
Now it's figuring out what's wrong and right.

Before it was things only for a child,
It was being the youngest of them all,
Now it is a party, and being wild,
Now it is social talks and a phone call.

Changes always happen so very fast.
I wish I could make every moment last.

               — *Alison Minam*

Sonnet

Why don't I join in, it's the thing to do,
sometimes it's tempting, that I must confess.
The things they say can throw my mind askew,
so those who pressure me hear this address.

Rap and baggy clothes are what suit you best.
The grunge world is the place where you should be.
Whether a flannel shirt or Paco vest,
what to wear is a choice that's made by me.

Just try one, it will give you a great rush.
Come on now, kid, don't you want to get high?
It would be great if these people would hush,
I'll do without the tar and cyanide.

I can only change myself for me,
I can not change for him or her or thee.

               — *Liam Moran*

2. SECOND SONNET

With the first homework assignment, you can simultaneously discuss the sonnets in Poems for Discussion, identifying the range of subjects poets have used and how the writers have resolved the tension or changed the direction of the discourse in the final sestet or couplet. From these and other sonnets, your class can generate a list of subjects from which students might choose one subject for a second sonnet. Some students might resist form and long to return to free verse. You might mention that "resistance to the form" could make a good subject for a sonnet. Students should choose one subject that has influenced their thinking and feelings, and then they should brainstorm ideas, images, and associations related to that particular subject. Have them find images to ground abstract ideas. Their notes should be developed and crafted into a sonnet. The drafts of the second sonnets can be read aloud in small groups.

3. CHOOSING AND REVISING

Once students have completed drafts of two sonnets, they can choose their favorite for a final revision, eventually to be included in a class anthology of writing. Your supportive criticism and that of student peers will motivate students to do the revisions necessary for success in this form. (See Revising Poetry in the Introduction.)

You could easily spend two or three weeks reading, discussing, writing, and revising sonnets. While students will be delighted to be released from the rigors of the form, their appreciation of the subtleties and power of the sonnet form to shape expression should grow immensely.

Student Examples

Some students are able to abide by all the constraints of the sonnet. Others master the intention or length or the rhyme scheme, but not the meter. These examples represent student efforts to integrate at least two or three sonnet requirements.

Skating

Gliding across the smooth white ice with grace,
A clean sheet of paper is marked with blades,
All dressed in fancy uniforms and lace
She swiftly turns in circles, then she fades.
She soars by as the wind blows quickly past.
She hangs up in the air with force and height
Until the music lets her down at last.
A smile sweeps o'er her face from left to right.
Her feeling of freedom builds up inside
She moves like swans gliding upon a lake
She skates across the ice full of pride
With pride she waves her hand with no mistake.

She leaves the ice filled with joy and glory
Her decorated paper now tells her story.

— *Shana Berger*

Writing

To me writing opens up a new door,
I get satisfied when a poem works,
Leads me through new worlds to explore
Some of my feelings and my thoughts.

You can write poems that get a smile on your face
Or about some feelings that come along
About the day you lost your sailing race
Or anger trying to explode so strong.

But writing sonnets ruins the whole notion.
It stops you from expressing yourself right
You don't have any power, any option,
Because the sonnet limits are so tight.

We struggle with the rhythm and the rhyme
To write a sonnet a second time.

— *Shiri Zilberman*

Magic and Pool

I put the chalk on the pool stick,
I scan the green, my best potential shot.
I call, "seven off the one ball," my trick.
I sink a cool spin-ball and now I'm hot!

My game goes bad and it's a losing streak,
The guy is slick, his cue is full of poise.
My chances are becoming dim and bleak.
My aim is numb, my ears are full of noise.

The tournament is near a lost home stretch.
My dream is gone and seems so out of reach.
A steady hand is best to make the catch.
If I could win, this—I will teach.

The game of pool is life without a fall,
To stay in front, not behind the "eight ball."

— *Zach Raemer*

Mattan, in his sonnet, speaks in the voice (persona) of the mother whose son has gone to war. The subjects of conflict and death are central to most older students who, like Mattan, are visiting from Israel or from other war-torn countries. The drama and abstraction of war make war a difficult subject for poetry. But the sonnet form, by its very constraints, eliminates unnecessary language and focuses the subject toward one event or thought. Mattan also uses slant rhyme ("stone" and "gone," and "friends" and "lands"). This gives him more latitude in searching for rhymes that do not sacrifice meaning. The use of irony adds power to the third quatrain, an effect he learned by reading Thomas Hardy's poem "The Man He Killed." His final line recalls Shelley's line "If Winter comes, can Spring be far behind?"—a poem he had studied in Israel.

The Mother Speaks

And then it came from up the street, a stone.
It slayed his heart, the one that loved just me.
It isn't true, please tell me he's not gone,
But no my heart is dead and so is he.

 I told him, "It is dangerous, so stay . . ."
But he said, "It's my duty, I must go"
I told him, "Please stay home . . ." he ran away,
I begged him to stay here, but he said, "No!"

And so he went and so he went to war
to kill the men who yesterday were friends.
He took his gun, his uniform he wore,
And went protecting nation, people, lands.

Up there, they say I'll meet him, he can't hide.
If he is gone, can I be far behind?

— *Mattan*

Not Enough Time to Praise the King

The time my class talked about Rodney King,
Was much too short to express all our thoughts.
My peers wore such faces of longing,
Who can explain why the police weren't caught.

No one would hear our so angry voices,
Who would care about our crying faces,
How could we help? What were our choices?
There was no justice in Rodney's cases.

We're all affected and feel the pain,
But fighting is not the best solution,
I mourn for all of those who were slain,
There is so much emotional pollution.

I hope my meaningful message is clear
That we don't have to wipe away our tears.

— *Amourence Mae En Lee*

Forbidden

Without the running river to pursue
the lonely fern holds only in himself
as he sadly wonders without a clue
that his loneliness is his only wealth

An arrow throught the heart of pain and love
was a blooming flower of desire
that one member was never dreaming of
while the other dwelled in love's passionate
fire

You reach for the close yet faraway sky
like you are swimming to no destiny
but in your hands never does that ocean lie
it moves to a nearby stone, without thee

Broken is a heart that was never whole
and now its fierce love has broken a soul.

— *Jess Auerbach*

Looking For Love

For many and many a year,
I've been looking in all the wrong places for love,
Looking around for someone to care,
Searching and searching low and above.

Finally, I've come up with just where to look,
I'd like to share with you what I've come up with.
First don't look in kitchens, for most boys don't cook,
But what I tell you is not just a myth.

Boys can be found in the strangest of places,
Beaches, clubs, skating rinks and schools,
Here you can find boys of all types and races,
But to find love you must follow my rules.

Don't be aggressive, take it slow, be patient.
Show him you're wonderful, beautiful, and radiant.

— *Angela Burke*

On Censorship, a Sonnet

Say anything you want if all can hear it,
But if they can't then lock it up inside.
The world may be disgusted by it, jeer it,
Or censor it 'til every bit has died.

Our laws of life say, "Go! Express yourself!"
"and do what ever it is you want to do!"
But do a wrong and you're back on the shelf,
And censorship has drawn your life for you.

All I ask is give someone a chance,
Don't turn away or censor what you find.
A picture, song, a poem or a dance.
Whatever it is, just let me speak my mind.

You can choose your liberty or your death.
But when freedom is cut off, then so is breath.

— *Jessica Ullian*

Final Thoughts About Death

Four or five times in the year when I just
relax and think, I find myself caught up
with these frightening thoughts of fog and dust.
Scary thoughts just fill my brain that once was
sharp
but now it's full of mystery and ideas so dark
about something feared and unknown,
important as a baby's birth but deadly as a shark,
final as a fatal rattlesnake crawling in the lawn.

I was trying very hard to find a name for Death,
Define this term, name the unstoppable end.
Many images came to my mind but none was
right.
At last I found my definition for this loss of
breath
to me. Death is a heavy, sealed wall of darkness
closing on the soul like a dull layer of coldness
and night.

— *Solomon*

4. VILLANELLE

Besides the sonnet, the villanelle and the
sestina are two additional forms that provide
intellectual challenge and the chance to integrate form and content. Both emerged during the Middle Ages in Europe as forms in which the troubadours conveyed their messages from village to village.

The villanelle evolved from an old Italian folk song. This structure was formalized by Jean Passerat in the 1500's. The villanelle is a cyclical form comprised of five three-line stanzas followed by one four-line stanza. It is based on two repeating lines: line one and line three of the first stanza alternate as last lines to succeeding stanzas. The final stanza uses both line one and line three as the final couplet. The poem uses two rhymes, A and B, and is usually in iambic pentameter, like the sonnet. The villanelle requires a subject that has a cyclical motif or an urgent message—material that will justify the repetitions. It requires a careful crafting of the two repeating lines so they deepen in meaning with each verse and have the flexibility of modifying the line or phrase before or after.

The most well-known villanelle in English is Dylan Thomas's "Do Not Go Gentle into That Good Night," which you will find under Poems for Discussion in Chapter 5. Notice the choice of simple rhyming words, while the meaning of the poem grows more complex and intense. The son's reoccurring admonition to his dying father to resist death grows more desperate as the poet acknowledges his need for a personal blessing or even curse from his father. Another familiar villanelle is Theodore Roethke's poem "The Waking." Elizabeth Bishop's villanelle "One Art" is a powerful, ironic poem about loss.

In "Birthmother," the unanswered questions of a daughter concerning her birth mother make use of the repeating lines of the villanelle form. There are some minor changes as the repeating lines reoccur. Sometimes a repeating line is combined with the preceding or following line (enjambment).

Birthmother

So child, there's a woman you've decided to claim
who deep in her belly and soul knows who you are.
Neither you nor I can know her name.

At times, she stops, wondering what you became.
She who birthed you, remembers and loves you from afar,
her child. There's a woman you've decided to claim

out of whose womb, pink and perfect, you came
to us. You call her Queen or Movie Star.
Neither you nor I can know her name.

And she was young, too young to blame
and fair and blue-eyed like you are
child. This woman you've decided to claim

was much too busy, you say. She had to deal with fame
and you're her princess, you bear the royal scar.
Neither you nor I can know her name.

Now she's like a distant flame
giving heat, pulling you towards her like a star.
Listen, child, the woman you've decided to claim . . .
Perhaps someday we will know her name.

— Judith Steinbergh

Poetry Exercise – Villanelle

Brainstorm a list of ideas that might suit the circular nature of the villanelle. Choose one of these, and for five minutes write your ideas that relate to the subject you have chosen. Make notes about what the focus or message of your poem will be. Write several attempts at a first verse. Decide which of the options offers the best lines one and three for alternating last lines in the remainder of the poem. Also consider the A and B rhyme, and rearrange or replace words so that you can stay with the rhyme scheme throughout the poem. Now, create a list of rhyming words on the A rhyme. Create a second list of rhyming words on the B rhyme. Use the alphabet to create these lists, and always consider one and multisyllable rhymes as well as slant rhymes.

Now, circle the words in your lists that might somehow relate to your topic. With these notes and resources, you can begin to draft a villanelle, using the form that follows and drawing on your ideas related to the topic, the focus or message you'd like to convey, and the appropriate rhyming words available. These multiple constraints make this form particularly challenging and satisfying. The limits also lead you to ideas and phrases that may surprise and delight you, as if the form itself were another mind participating in the creative process. Crafting is a large part of this poem, and you will need to make several drafts to refine the language and make the rhythm of the poem musical and close to natural language. Try to make the grammar of the poem as close to natural speech as possible. Read the poem aloud to yourself many times. This will help you hear where a word might be replaced or a rhythm smoothed out.

Villanelle Form

Directions: Write a villanelle with meter that approximates iambic pentameter, -/-/-/-/-/.

_____ A/1

_____ B

_____ A/2

_____ A

_____ B

_____ A/1

_____ A

_____ B

_____ A/2

_____ A

_____ B

_____ A/1

_____ A

_____ B

_____ A/2

_____ A

_____ B

_____ A/1

_____ A/2

Student Examples

The villanelle allowed this student to say something important about her alienation from her peers, and it allowed her to say it over and over—a way to think it through and move toward a resolution.

Villanelle

I have this problem with kids my own age,
we can't cope with each other at all.
I feel when I do things I'm forced on a stage.

My problem is hard and it can cause rage.
If we could just talk then I think we shall
change this problem I have with kids my own age.

But years later, I hope to be sage,
because that means to be wise and be tall;
Maybe some day there will be no stage.

I feel like an animal alone in a cage,
but if I'm strong all the way I'll be tall.
How will I solve this problem with kids my own age.

But they will change after years and with age,
so will I and then I do think I will give them a call.
I feel when I do things I'm forced on a stage.

Some day maybe I could make this a page
in a book, for the things I recall.
And maybe this problem I have with kids of my age,
will be gone and so will the stage.

— *Sargeant Donovan-Smith*

It is hard for students to meet all of the requirements of this form. Sargeant grasped the repetition and rhyme patterns, used very sophisticated enjambment, where sentences flow from one line to the next, but her rhythms were inconsistent. Students may succeed in repeating the appropriate lines but abandon the rhyme scheme. However, any aspect of the form that is internalized will deepen the student's understanding of poetry.

B-jorn, an urban eighth-grader, used only the stanza requirements and two rhymes for this variation on a villanelle. The confinement of even this loose concept of the villanelle helps B-jorn focus his story and his frustration.

No Movement No Life Shot Dead

No movement No life Shot dead
You woke up rolling in money
And you go to sleep with a bullet in your head.

Learning how to steal but not how to read
Going through life thinking everything's funny
You died on a high from crack, heroin, or speed.

"I'm gonna stop" are words you often said,
You played your parents for dummies,
But they were right when they said you need
    an education to succeed.

You say drugs make you feel invincible and are
    something you need,
But when you got shot you cried to your mummy,
Maybe you'd be alive if it wasn't for your greed.

You have a gang that you lead,
You went downtown to buy a chain for
    your honey,
You got her pregnant and now you have another
    mouth to feed.

When the gun was pointed to your head,
    you pled,
You didn't listen to your parents, now who's the
    real dummy?
After you were dead, your killer fled,
And there you lie, No Movement No life
    Shot dead.

— *B-jorn*

What If the World Were Only Black and White?

What if the world were only black and white?
The thought stays in my mind and never fades
I wonder and imagine the weird sight.

The flowers would be ugly and not bright,
Making the picture all ugly and frayed.
Only if the world were just black and white.

My lovely, luxuriant, light green kite
Would not have its lush green color of jade
I wonder and imagine this weird sight.

Thinking of the sky, black or white, gives a fright,
Because then the sunset would be made
Of only two colors which are black and white.

The leaves would fall with no color or might
Since they'd have no bright colors to display.
I wonder and imagine this weird sight.

But the good thing is there would be no fight
Over what color is best. But the thought never fades
About the world being only black and white.
I wonder and imagine this weird sight.

— *Lynn Y. Choi*

Computers

Access, process, compute, store;
there are so many things they can do.
With one you're able to do so much more.

Sometimes life can be such a bore,
but at the screen I'm never blue.
Access, process, compute, store.

Colors and games like I've never seen pour
out on the screen. They're just machines, says who?
With one, you're able to do so much more.

"Oddell Lake," "Oregon Trail," "Tetris," "Games
of War:"

they're exciting and suspenseful too.
Access, process, compute, store.

Every night you'll find my homework on the
monitor,
I won't even bother with pens, it's true.
With one you're able to do so much more.

Having a computer opens new doors,
every day you can learn something new.
Access, process, compute, store,
with one you're able to do so much more.

— *Eric Simundza*

Forest of Darkness

Whispers of sorrow echo through the night,
the darkness silently cries out in pain,
All hope is gone; it vanished like the light.

Through the darkness my mind runs wild
with fright,
The night is mine alone; I've made my claim.
Whispers of sorrow echo through the night.

Sadness has gone but my anger is bright,
I violently search for someone to blame.
All hope is gone; it vanished like the light.

Trees glare down at me from their looming
height,
anger stares at me like a blazing flame,
whispers of sorrow echo through the night.

I clench my fists tightly with all my might,
tears drop silently like the night rain,
hope is gone; it vanished like the light.

The coal-black darkness and grief, strain
my sight,
the depth of my anguish I cannot name.
Whispers of sorrow echo through the night,
all hope is gone, it vanished like the light.

— *Jenny Lusk-Yablick*

5. SESTINA

The sestina was attributed to Arnaut Daniel, a troubadour poet of the Middle Ages. It was refined by Dante and Petrarch in Italy and other poets through the ages. As its name hints, the sestina is based on sixes (from the Latin, *sextus*) and has six unrhymed stanzas of six lines each. The words at the ends of the first stanza's lines reappear at the ends of all the other lines. The sestina concludes with a three-line stanza (tercet) that uses all six end words—two to a line. In contrast to the villanelle, the sestina is a long form and provides space for an in-depth exploration of a subject important to the writer. The length and repeated words tend to create a little story.

In a sestina, the six end words of the first verse are repeated in a prescribed order, each new stanza derived from the previous stanza: the first end word of stanza two becomes the last end word of stanza one; the second end word of stanza two becomes the first end word of stanza one; the third end word of stanza two becomes the second-to-last end word of stanza one; and so on. Although the final tercet in a classical sestina would use the order of ABCDEF, two words per line, contemporary poets have taken liberties with the order. Three wonderful examples of the sestina are "Sestina," by Elizabeth Bishop, "Shadows," by Linda Pastan, and "Here in Katmandu," by Donald Justice.

In Judith Steinbergh's sestina "Talking Physics with My Son," which follows, the son's orbiting of the kitchen table and Albert Einstein's equation are integral to the inter weaving of words in the form. Notice that the six end words of her first verse—man, gravity, space, light, son, time—are repeated following the sestina form, with some variations. For example, "son" in the first verse, line five becomes "sun" in verse three, line si; "gravity" later becomes "grave" and "engraved"; and "man" transforms at the very end into "amen."

Talking Physics with My Son

David reads the sports page holding it up like a man
and to the side of his French toast plate with a gravity
that makes me smile. His compact body defines his space.
Watching football on t.v., in the pale violet light,
he shouts, his fist punching the air. After school, my son
lies in the dirt shooting marbles or runs against his record time,

yet pronouncing his French, he sits in my lap. What a time!
Ten. A treasure stumbled over in the midst of a woman's
life. A flame inside beveled glass pushing at the night, a son
orbiting me and this table where I sit as if our mutual gravity
would keep him circling forever, pulsing with some inner light.
You know the way young boys can't stop moving when they talk, they space

out, jiggle like molecules, hang from doorways, legs dangling in space,
chattering about energy and mass, e=mc^2, how time
is relative, can't be counted on to proceed in a line, and light,
the only constant in our lives, more constant than women or men,
can actually be bent from its path by gravity
so *where* we see the stars is distorted by the mass of the sun

in fact, how he and I observe a star, or galaxy, or sun
may differ depending on our speed or where we are in space.
As I said, it's all relative! Moreover, gravity
not only pulls our blood and tugs at tides, but slows down time.
Flowers grow—iron rusts more slowly and if David manned
a spaceship traveling the universe near the speed of light,

he might reach Andromeda, discover new life, alight
on a green lush planet, looking back at our own faint sun
and a white-haired mother while he remains a young man.
How this child is seen, how he proceeds through life, his space-
time continuum, the path he takes . . . only time
will tell. I might bend him towards me a bit with my gravity.

The shortest path between birth and the carved date on the grave
is not always what it seems. Divergence, enlightenment,
intervene, pushing out the edges of the mind. One at a time,
revelations unfold in this small tired boy. It's late, the sun
has set already, all this heady conversation, this space-
talk, this avid fascination with a brilliant man

is engraved on us like an equation. Pull the quilt up, son.
I'll turn out the light. You're drowsy, but your mind still speeds through space.
It's time for sleep. Thank you God or Einstein for this child. Amen.

— *Judith Steinbergh*

In Fredric Lown's "Sestina for a Grande Dame," the six end words are "family," "world," "focus," "stories," "power," and "lives." These words do not vary from verse to verse, although the verb tenses do change.

Allow your students flexibility in writing this difficult and intellectually challenging form.

Sestina for a Grande Dame

She was always the Grande Dame of our family
   realm, ruling from the regal heights of a former world.
   It was vanishing, she feared, so she tried to focus
   our mundane visons on allegories and stories,
   (of her uncle from Berlin who bought her trousseau), giving power
   to her claims that she was a voice in our lives.

We knew her in our life, not the many lives
   she had already lived with her family
   in cities and villages and towns where the power
   resided in an affluent language our world
   does not speak and will not learn so stories
   remain buried beneath layers of lenses out of focus.

She commanded through her presence that the present focus
   on the past, that her children's children's lives
   remember their heritage through her stories
   about a time when sacrifice secured family
   values of unity and spirituality in a world
   that was losing its center through its abuse of power.

We understood that her source of power
   was in her uncanny ability to focus
   our sights, if only fleetingly, into her world
   of backs bent over books and female hands with lives
   of their own encircling candles that gave light to family
   memory collectively created to pass on her stories.

She never forgot a detail as she sifted stories
   like sand through hands that had once held power
   in a Polish shtetl on the German border where her family
   life centered around her holy father whose prayers focused
   on searching eyes imprisoned in gaunt bodies and tattered lives,
   but his attentions rested on her. He was her world.

We were humbled by her blend of the simple with her world
   wiseness that yielded recipes for stories
   so rich in taste that our own lives
   became bland, not by her design, by our loss of power
   in a culture committed to sound-bites of unfocused
   rage compelling us to seek solace in our family.

She regaled us with fables of her old world family
   but pierced our souls with poignant stories focusing
   her breath on her second life and giving power to our lives.
                                                    — *Fredric Lown*

Poetry Exercise – Sestina

You might begin by choosing a topic and generating ten or twelve end words related to it. Make sure that a few of these words are concrete (physical) and that one or two might function as various parts of speech (a noun, verb, adjective, etc.). Draft a first stanza and see which six of these end words might be most useful or interesting. Another approach is to think of a topic and just begin writing and see what words appear at the end of the first six lines. You can adjust your line breaks after writing a first stanza to place strong words in the end-word positions. A third, more gamelike approach to beginning a sestina is to write six end words on a piece of paper and exchange with a friend in class. Here you have the mind of another superimposed on your thinking and personal style. Once you have chosen your end words, write down all the remaining end words in correct rotation at the far right of the page on the following form. Then you won't have to worry about the order as you are writing. You will be amazed at how your thinking shifts as you approach the next end word. It is like constructing a web where the shape is forecast, but the precise nature of what you will catch is a mystery.

Sestina Form

Directions: Choose your six end words and write them down at the far right, using the letters A to F. Then write a sestina.

Stanza 1 _____ A

_____ B

_____ C

_____ D

_____ E

_____ F

Stanza 2 _____ F

_____ A

_____ E

_____ B

_____ D

_____ C

Stanza 3 _____ C

_____ F

_____ D

_____ A

_____ B

_____ E

Name _____ Date _____

Sestina Form (*continued*)

Stanza 4 _____ E

_____ C

_____ B

_____ F

_____ A

_____ D

Stanza 5 _____ D

_____ E

_____ A

_____ C

_____ F

_____ B

Stanza 6 _____ B

_____ D

_____ F

_____ E

_____ C

_____ A

Final Tercet _____ AB

_____ CD

_____ EF

Student Examples

For Dad, a Sestina.

In the bottom of the box in the back of the dark closet,
I found the hidden album with the forbidden picture.
So statuesque and unreal; too young to be Mom and Dad.
With things the way they are now, I can't imagine them in love.
I don't remember much; I only lived with Dad for three years.
Here they look like dolls, dressed up and empty.

I take all the pictures out until the album is empty.
I put the album at the bottom, shove the box to the back of the closet
and shut the door; just like you shut me out years
ago. I have a piece of your past in this picture.
The evidence of a young beardless face, superficially in love.
This man that my older siblings knew and called, "Dad."

Watching from my window I would wait for "Daddy"
to come in the "Orange Pumpkin," the big empty
van, to take me and Jen and Pete for a visit. I loved
going to visit. While Dad played ball with Pete, I would open the game closet,
and amuse myself hoping that someone would look at the picture
I drew or play Candyland with me. I would wait for what seemed like years.

And I feel like I'm still waiting and now it really has been years.
Always hoping that you'll care, that you'll become "Dad."
Maybe you care in your own way, but I just can't picture
you ever being able to care enough to fill that empty
void you created when you left. Way back in the closet
of my mind, I remember always wanting your love.

Now when I see you, we smile and laugh and share a common love
for your new sons, my half brothers. Despite the years
of difference in age, Nathaniel, Ben and I get along well. You put me in the closet
you call a room, and I pretend I don't mind, Dad.
You say you want me to feel like it's home, but I feel empty.
You have a new family, and I just can't fit into that picture.

With your new camera you'll take my picture,
hang it on your office wall to show everyone you love
all your children, but when you look at the wall the picture frame is empty.
We can go on pretending for years and years,
but you're not fooling me, I know how you feel Dad.
It's just too bad that you're not able to "come out of your closet."

I'll go and put the pictures back in the closet.
I know that for you Dad, it's not easy to show love.
And that's why all these years, it's really you who's been empty.

— *Ingrid Goldfein*

This sestina was written by Jennie Garver using ends words chosen by a classmate.

The Trestle

Harsh words, maddening thoughts, angry fights based on your ignorance.
You always provoked hatred. I knew the truth behind it all; you were the charlatan.
When I needed love and help, someone to be like a trestle
for me, the house was empty as my world. You would always betray
my trust, leave me. My heart would grow back and you would kill it, a holocaust
of my once-love for you. Your sparkling sapphire

eyes would laugh at me. Uncaring and cold is sapphire
and so were you. I had once thought I loved you. Ignorance.
Now I feel alone, unwanted, a child of the holocaust.
And you sit there and laugh at my needs, a charlatan
of the difference between love and hate. Now I will betray
you. I am leaving, taking with me the legs of the trestle

that has held you up so long. You will find another trestle.
You will lure her like you did me. Promise her the sapphire
ocean and emeral earth. You will swear never to betray
her and she will give you her heart in open hands, ignorant.
Then she will learn what it means to love a charlatan
and liar. During the long cold lonely nights she will wish for a holocaust

to kill off your coldness and bring in the warm
afternoons with you when a holocaust
is the farthest from her mind. She will become another crippled trestle,
ready to be thrown out. I am no longer a charlatan
to pain and misery. In the beginning I was out in search of sapphire
or gold, and I though I had found them in you. Ignorance.
I knew inside you was fool's gold, nothing more. But my heart betrayed

my brain, unbelieving. It told me to stay until it, too, was betrayed
in this exposed battered state. I am a cat. The holocaust
you call love took eight of my lives. I am ready to live again in ignorance,
start over and forget you as you forgot me. This trestle
is gone, gone to look for someone who is willing to find the sapphire
that still exists in me despite you. He will be no charlatan

to my past. He will hear about the infamous charlatan,
YOU! He will promise never to make me betray
any emotion save joy. He will state his love in phrases beautiful as sapphire.
In loving me, he will poke through debris from the holocaust
you left in me, the open wounds present from being nothing but a trestle
for you. He will wonder how my heart could be so ignorant

but he won't judge. I want you to know I'm leaving you, no longer a charlatan
to how I feel. I know you won't feel hurt or betrayed.
In parting, I hope one day you will find one you do love, the right trestle.

                                                              — *Jennie Garver*

Chapter 8

Praise Poems and Odes

Introduction

In contrast to the flat or ironic tone of the protest poem or the confined and rigorous forms of the sonnet, villanelle, and sestina, is a much less restrained style of poetry that we call poem of praise. The poem of praise contains a lushness of language or a piling up of images, a great exuberance for the subject, even exaggeration. The poet may use elevated language and/or the form of address (ode) to heighten the adulation. The idea is to convey the intensity of the feeling with specific language, as opposed to abstraction.

An ode is an ancient form, a song (from the Greek word *aeidein*—to sing) invented by Pindar nearly 2,500 years ago that exalts and often addresses a person or a thing. Pindar's victory odes, which celebrated the victors of athletic competitions, were formal in structure, meter, and stanzaic pattern. Horace (first century B.C.), Keats, Shelley, and Wordsworth stayed within particular rules of form and praised dignified themes. In more recent literature, poets have discarded many aspects of formality and structure but have kept the intensity and sense of exaltation. Pablo Neruda, in his *Odas Elementales (Odes to Simple Things)*, uses exalted, spontaneous language to celebrate ordinary objects: lemons, watermelons, fleas, socks, and such.

Poems for Discussion

1. Song of Myself
(*excerpts*)

1

I celebrate myself, and sing myself,
And what I assume you shall assume,
For every atom belonging to me as good belongs to you.

I loaf and invite my soul,
I lean and loaf at my ease observing a spear of summer grass.

My tongue, every atom of my blood, form'd from this soil, this air,
Born here of parents born here from parents the same, and their parents the same,
I, now thirty-seven years old in perfect health begin,
Hoping to cease not till death.
Creeds and schools in abeyance,
Retiring back a while suffced at what they are, but never forgotten,
I harbor for good or bad, I permit to speak at every hazard,
Nature without check with original energy.

31

I believe a leaf of grass is no less than the journeywork of the stars,
And the pismire is equally perfect, and a grain of sand, and the egg of the wren,
And the tree-toad is a chef-d'oeuvre for the highest,
And the running blackberry would adorn the parlors of heaven,
And the narrowest hinge in my hand puts to scorn all machines,
And the cow crunching with depress'd head surpasses any statue,
And a mouse is miracle enough to stagger sextillions of infidels.
I find I incorporate gneiss, coal, long-threaded moss, fruits, grains, succulent roots,
And am stucco'd with quadrupeds and birds all over,
And have distanced what is behind me for good reasons,

But call any thing back again when I desire it.

In vain the speeding or shyness,
In vain the plutonic rocks send their old heat against my approach,
In vain the mastodon retreats beneath its own powder'd bones,
In vain objects stand leagues off and assume manifold shapes,
In vain the ocean settling in hollows and the great monsters lying low,
In vain the buzzard houses herself with the sky,
In vain the snake slides through the creepers and logs,
In vain the elk takes to the inner passes of the woods,
In vain the razor-bill'd auk sails far north to Labrador,
I follow quickly, I ascent to the nest in the fissure of the cliff.

— *Walt Whitman*

2. Phenomenal Woman

Pretty women wonder where my secret lies.
I'm not cute or built to suit a fashion model's size
But when I start to tell them,
They think I'm telling lies.
I say,
It's in the reach of my arms,
The span of my hips,
The stride of my step,
The curl of my lips.
I'm a woman
Phenomenally.
Phenomenal woman,
That's me.

I walk into a room
Just as cool as you please,
And to a man,
The fellows stand or
Fall down on their knees.
Then they swarm around me,
A hive of honey bees.
I say,
It's the fire in my eyes,
And the flash of my teeth,
The swing of my waist,
And the joy in my feet.
I'm a woman
Phenomenally.
Phenomenal woman,
That's me.

Men themselves have wondered
What they see in me.
They try so much

But they can't touch
My inner mystery.
When I try to show them
They say they still can't see.
I say,
It's in the arch of my back,
The sun of my smile,
The ride of my breasts,
The grace of my style.
I'm a woman
Phenomenally.
Phenomenal woman,
That's me.

Now you understand
Just why my head's not bowed.
I don't shout or jump about
Or have to talk real loud.
When you see me passing
It ought to make you proud.
I say,
It's in the click of my heels,
The bend of my hair,
The palm of my hand,
The need for my care.
'Cause I'm a woman
Phenomenally.
Phenomenal woman,
That's me.

— *Maya Angelou*

3. For My People

For my people everywhere singing their slave songs
     repeatedly: their dirges and their ditties and their
     blues and jubilees, praying their prayers nightly
     to an unknown god, bending their knees humbly
     to an unseen power;

For my people lending their strength to the years, to
     the gone years and the now years and the maybe
     years, washing ironing cooking scrubbing sewing
     mending hoeing plowing digging planting pruning
     patching dragging along never gaining never reap-
     ing never knowing and never understanding;

For my playmates in the clay and dust and sand of
     Alabama backyards playing baptizing and preach-
     ing and doctor and jail and soldier and school and
     mama and cooking and playhouse and concert and
     store and hair and Miss Choomby and company;

For the cramped bewildered years we went to school
     to learn to know the reasons why and the answers
     to and the people who and the places where and
     the days when, in memory of the bitter hours
     when we discovered we were black and poor and
     small and different and nobody cared and nobody
     wondered and nobody understood;

For the boys and girls who grew in spite of these things
     to be man and woman to laugh and dance and
     sing and play and drink their wine and religion
     and success, to marry their playmates and bear
     children and then die of consumption and anemia
     and lynching;

For my people thronging 47th Street in Chicago and
     Lenox Avenue in New York and Rampart Street
     in New Orleans, lost disinherited dispossessed and
     happy people filling the cabarets and taverns and
     other people's pockets needing bread and shoes
     and milk and land and money and something—
     something all our own;

For my people walking blindly spreading joy, losing
     time being lazy, sleeping when hungry, shouting
     when burdened, drinking when hopeless, tied and
     shackled among ourselves by the
     unseen creatures who tower over us omnisciently
     and laugh;

For my people blundering and groping and floundering
     in the dark of churches and schools and clubs

and societies, associations and councils and com-
mittees and conventions, distressed and disturbed
and deceived and devoured by money-hungry
glory-craving leeches, preyed on by facile force of
state and fad and novelty, by false prophet and
holy believer;

For my people standing staring trying to fashion a
better way from confusion, from hypocrisy and
misunderstanding, trying to fashion a world that
will hold all the people, all the faces, all the adams
and eves and their countless generations;

Let a new earth rise. Let another world be born. Let a
bloody peace be written in the sky. Let a second
generation full of courage issue forth; let a people
loving freedom come to growth. Let a beauty full
of healing and a strength of final clenching be the
pulsing in our spirits and our blood. Let the
martial songs be written, let the dirges disappear.
Let a race of men now rise and take control.

— *Margaret Walker*

4. Gold

Suddenly all the gold I ever wanted
Let loose and fell on me. A storm of gold
Starting with rain a quick sun catches falling
And in the rain (fall within fall) a whirl
Of yellow leaves, glitter of paper nuggets.

And there were puddles the sun was winking at
And fountains saucy with gold fish, fantails,
    sunfish,
And trout slipping in streams it would be insult
To call gold and, trailing their incandescent
Fingers, meteors and a swimming moon.

Flowers of course. Chrysanthemums and clouds
Of twisted cool with-hazel and marigolds,
Late dandelions and all the goldenrods.
And bees all pollen and honey, wasps
    gold-banded

And hornets dangling their legs, cruising
    the sun.

The luminous birds, goldfinches and orioles,
Were gone or going, leaving some of their gold
Behind in near-gold, off-gold, ultra-golden
Beeches, birches, maples, apples. And under
The appletrees the lost, the long-lost names.

Bumpkins and squashes heaped in a cold-gold
    sunset—
Oh, I was crushed like Croesus, Midas-smothered
And I died in a maple-fall a boy was raking
Nightward to burst all bonfire-gold together—
And leave at last in a thin blue prayer of smoke.

— *Robert Francis*

5. Ode to My Socks

Maru Mori brought me
a pair
of socks
knitted with her own
shepherd's hands,
two socks soft
as rabbits.
I slipped
my feet into them
as if
into
jewel cases
woven
with threads of
dusk
and sheep's wool.

Audacious socks,
my feet became
two woolen
fish,
two long sharks
of lapis blue
shot
with a golden thread.
two mammoth blackbirds.
two cannons,
thus honored
were
my feet
by
these
celestial
socks.
They were
so beautiful
that for the first time
my feet seemed
unaceptable to me,
two tired old
fire fighters
not worthy
of the woven
fire
of those luminous
socks.

Nonetheless,
I resisted
the strong temptation
to save them
the way schoolboys
bottle
fireflies,
the way scholars
hoard
sacred documents.
I resisted
the wild impulse
to place them
in a cage
of gold
and daily feed them
birdseed
and rosy melon flesh.
Like explorers
who in the forest
surrender a rare
and tender deer
to the spit
and eat it
with remorse,
I stuck out
my feet
and pulled on
the
handsome
socks,
and
then my shoes.

So this is
the moral of my ode:
twice beautiful
is beauty
and what is good doubly
good
when it is a case of two
woolen socks
in wintertime.

— *Pablo Neruda*

6. When I Dance

When I dance it isn't merely
That music absorbs my shyness,
My laughter settles in my eyes,
My swings of arms convert my frills
As timing tunes my feet with floor
As if I never just looked on.

It is that when I dance
O music expands my hearing
And it wants no mathematics,
It wants no thinking, no speaking,
It only wants all my feeling
In with animation of place.

When I dance it isn't merely
That surprises dictate movements,
Other rhythms move my rhythms,
I uncradle rocking-memory
And skipping, hopping and running
All mix movements I balance in.

It is that when I dance
I'm costumed in a rainbow mood,
I'm okay at any angle,
Outfit of drums crowds madness round,
Talking winds and plucked strings conspire,
Beat after beat warms me like sun.

When I dance it isn't merely
I shift bodyweight balances
As movement amasses my show,
I celebrate each dancer here,
No sleep invades me now at all
And I see how I am tireless.

It is that when I dance
I gather up all my senses
Well into hearing and feeling,
With body's flexible postures
Telling their poetry in movement
And I celebrate all rhythms.

— *James Berry*

7. Across Nebraska

Thank you God for this dome of sky, for clouds brushing the tops
of corn, for the nurse telling Alvin who lives in the Bronx
that farmers feed corn-tops to cows, and how she grew up "right
over there," pointing out the window of the bus, "about fifty
or so miles." Thank you for these trails across the prairie,
the same trails wagons made, now paved, for us, for this Trailways
bus, for all these people talking about Iowa, Ohio, Colorado,
how it is where I live, in Lincoln, Toledo, Sioux City,
Grand Junction. Thank you for this country and the people

in it, Jeff on leave from the Army, Lois going home to Idaho,
Martin and Malcolm going to visit Grandmother, the little boy
standing in the aisle next to me saying, "You uh ole Coke bottle
is whut you is," laughing and patting my arm with both his hands,
slapping out the rhythm of "You uh olde tire swing out in thuh yard,
a trash can top use for a helmet." Thank you for this boy and his
song out of the blue, for Beethoven and Sony, for the 6th Symphony
over and over from Grand Central Station to Castro Street across
this country of blue sky and Alabama cotton ball white clouds.

Thank you for telephone poles whizzing by, for rolled up hay
on the ground, a white cow and her calf, the head-set I'm wearing
and the miracle it is. Thank you for these bridal satin white
clouds painted on Japanese silk screen of periwinkle blue sky,
for the rush of Nebraska, these fields rushing by, for paved roads
through green woods, silos, mud, mothers combing children's hair,

black walnut trees, three rows of corn in a front yard, an old
barn leaning to one side, a chicken coop painted red, and five
children playing Peas Porridge Hot on this bus right now.

Thank you for sky as blue as true blue, as blue as a first prize
ribbon for the best peach pie at the county Fair for these powdered
sugar clouds, these butter frosting clouds, these best white cake
and icing clouds, for Beethoven and children laughing, for this
Trailways bus, this day in July, for the cottony soft comforting
white flannel blanket clouds, for air conditioning, Cokes, potato
chips, people, Pepsi cups, ice, lined sheets of paper and a good pen,
for Greg, Robin and Pat, for Gin Rummy, for the little girl crawling
under my knees, for Teresa and her two children three rows up,

for Mother Teresa, for Sister Teresa, for Saint Teresa who said
"God, You know my heart," for the young man in the back in black
leather and chains, tattoos on both arms, who stood up and took off
his reflecting sun-glasses fifty miles out of Chicago to say, "God!
this is beautiful! This is my country!" Thank you for these Queen
Anne's lace clouds, these dandelion puff clouds, these Bing Crosby
priest movie clouds, these Little House on the Prairie childhood
clouds, these fairy-tale, story-book, happy ending clouds with real
true silver linings, and for the dome of the cornflower blue Nebraska sky.

— *Deanna Mason*

8. Jazz Fantasia

Drum on your drums, batter on your banjos,
sob on the long cool winding saxophones.
Go to it, O jazzmen.

Sling your knuckles on the bottoms of the happy
tin pans, let your trombones ooze, and go husha-
husha-hush with the slippery sandpaper.

Moan like an autumn wind high in the lonesome treetops, moan soft like
you wanted somebody terrible, cry like a racing car slipping away from a
motorcycle cop, bang-bang! you jazzmen, bang altogether drums, traps,
banjos, horns, tin cans—make two people fight on the top of a stairway
and scratch each other's eyes in a clinch tumbling down the stairs.

Can the rough stuff . . . Now a Mississippi steamboat pushes up the night
river with a hoo-hoo-hoo-oo . . . and the green lanterns calling to the high
soft stars . . . a red moon rides in the humps of the low river hills . . .
go to it, O jazzmen.

— *Carl Sandburg*

Questions for Discussion and Analysis

1. What is the tone and diction in Walt Whitman's "Song of Myself"? How does the title itself indicate a break from traditional English content and form? What patterns and rhythms in Whitman's phrasing become evident as the poem progresses? What biblical and classical rhetorical techniques emerge in section 31 of "Song of Myself"? How does Whitman inflate and shape his own self-image? Does this empower the reader in any way?

2. Maya Angelou's "Phenomenal Woman" is also a celebration of self, a variety of a boasting or a brag poem. (See Chapter 3, section 4.) How does the poet use rhythm and line break to mirror the strut of a person filled with confidence? Read sections aloud as you stride around the room. Give examples of repetition, boasting, exaggeration, inflated language, and the accumulation of images. How does diction and intonation make this poem accessible to young people in the current culture? What poetic techniques does Angelou use that differ from those Walt Whitman uses? In what ways are these two poems similar?

3. In Margaret Walker's poem "For My People," her praise is outer directed. What is the obvious structure for shaping and giving the poem momentum? What do you notice about sentences and punctuation? What religious and political orators do you know who have used these techniques of repetition and parallel structure (Frederick Douglass, Martin Luther King, Jr., John F. Kennedy, Jesse Jackson)?

4. In Robert Francis's praise of "Gold," he draws on a profusion of images from nature which evoke "gold," whole stanzas to extol flowers, insects, birds, and vegetables. How many times does the word "gold" appear either alone or in compound words? What is the effect of this chiming of the color over and over in the poem? Find a copy of the poem "Pied Beauty," by Gerard Manley Hopkins. How is the diction and imagery in the Francis poem reminiscent of the Hopkins poem?

5. In "Ode to My Socks" poet Pablo Neruda elevates "socks" to an exalted level. Identify all the descriptive imagery that shows this elevation. Why does Neruda use humorous exaggeration throughout the poem, only to return to mundane reality in the conclusion of the poem? Why would a poet choose "socks" to praise? Have you ever felt so exuberant toward a piece of clothing—an old sweater or pair of jeans, a treadless pair of sneakers?

6. James Berry, writing from his Caribbean experience in "When I Dance," praises the transformation he undergoes when he is dancing. How does he describe the changes he experiences? How do sound and motion images convey his feelings about dancing? How does the poet personify music? What are its demands? What powers besides motion does the music have over him? Give an instance of elevated language. What happens to the normal logic of the language itself as the writer is consumed by the feelings of dancing? What rhythmic techniques does this poem share with "Phenomenal Woman"?

7. Deanna Mason's poem "Across Nebraska" borrows its opening line from E.E. Cummings's poem, "i thank you god for most this amazing . . . . Discuss the techniques she uses in light of what you have learned from previous examples in the discussion poems. How is the length of the bus ride across America linked to the form in which she writes the poem? What specific events does she describe that re-create the flavor of this bus ride for the reader? How do humor, irony, overstatement, and elevation of language influence the reader's feeling toward America?

8. In "Jazz Fantasia," who is Carl Sandburg celebrating? What rhythms has he chosen to imitate the instruments and musical style he praises? How does the imperative mode change the tone of the poem from what it might be if it were a mere description? How does the prose-poem style (absence of line breaks) relate to the music and environment Sandburg honors?

Bibliography of Additional Poems and Books

"Ain't That Bad," Maya Angelou

"Pied Beauty" (and others), Gerard Manley Hopkins

Odas Elementales, Pablo Neruda

Neighborhood Odes, Gary Soto

"Fern Hill," Dylan Thomas

"Ode on a Grecian Urn," John Keats

"My Heart Leaps Up," and "Ode: Intimations of Immortality from Recollections of Early Childhood," William Wordsworth

Writing Exercise

Poetry Exercise – Praise Poems

Choose a topic for which you have considerable enthusiasm or passion. This might include a sport, an art form, a particular talent, a pet, a favorite family member, an old sweater, a journey, a place you visit, a type of weather, or yourself. Try to describe your feelings toward that subject by gathering images, making them more and more extreme, building up momentum through rhythms or repetitions or through the use of exaggeration. You might try this exercise in the form of a prose poem where line breaks are unspecified or in the form of an ode.

Student Examples

Play

When I play
the music surrounds me.
My golden trumpet making sweet sounds in the air
my heart spills out.
Wedged comfortably between two others of my kind,
I hear them join me.
intertwining
embracing
running
dancing
While we sit still in the hot room.
The sound of the band is purple
a rich, thick sound filled with heart
soul
and we move on to rainbows as we start to end the piece.
Another gold and I hold hands in a duet.
We fly and dip
sadly, joyfully, crazily
sharing each other as we play the same sounds.
A vibrating silver pierces the thick air
and children who haven't been listening
have to look up
when we play.

— *Lillie S. Marshall*

Art

Art melts in my hand
it cruises along the rough board,
it digs into the canvas with delight,
it runs like a stream or a meadow
blowing in the wind,
it coughs and splatters and finds one's destiny,
it pinches,
it writes,
it collapses onto the paper or canvas,
it moans and cries,
it laughs and lies,
when it moves, it slides.
It is a flower on a summer day,
with a touch of bright red.
it stands out with glee
when it rides the waves of the sea,
it can be used so differently,
Art saves the world from its agony.

— *Sarah Bernice Weintraub*

My Poems

I am a rainbow poet sitting in the deep sky
upon a rainbow creating magical and mystical
poems. My poems then seep into the cracks
of the earth and fill them with color.

I am a thunder poet walking through a storm
making loud images in my head
to turn into a poem.

I am a rhythm poet riding a seahorse
in a blue green lagoon writing poems
as I listen to the
currents of the water. Then slowly
my poems crawl and play with the sand.

I am a poet.

I am a poet upon the moon
writing mysterious silver poems
as I look back to the earth and wonder.

I am a sun poet walking on a golden bridge
of light writing warm glowing poems.
My poems are then separated and come alive.

I am a poet that blooms with the flowers
dreaming on a silky rose petal of memories.
I am a people poet making my way
through a storm in a city
while thinking of writing a
poem about feelings.

I am a poet.

— *Linh O.*

Ode to Colors

Without bright, shining colors the world
    would be but a bleak dismal dungeon.
Without colors there would be no need
    to draw or paint
Or stay out an extra hour
    to watch the golden sunset.
There would be no reason to wait for spring
And run through a lush green field
    picking the purple violet
And drinking the sweet golden nectar
    from the pink honeysuckle.
There would be no color for the halos of angels
    or for the tail of Satan.
There would be no color for the dark eyes
    of the raven or for the lucky rainbow.
There would be no need to make large bouquets
    of wildflowers for your mother.

There would be no reason to wear
    matching socks
Or go to the seashore to collect shells.
Without colors there would be
    no shiny red apples for the teachers.

— *Kate Latson*

Ode to Merengue

Merengue,
I feel my body move to the beat,
The natural sounds of the instruments
get my body in motion.
The rhythm of the music keeps my
body out of control.
In the morning, noon, and night,
I listen to the sounds of the conga drums,
organs, horns, and many more instruments
that fill my heart with soul.

— *Mercedes María Molina*

In Praise of Dance

A Dance of Love . . .
of curving elbows and circling shoulders and
open palms and parted lips, whispering stones
of sunrise and midnight and ocean and lilac dreams,
A Dance of Passion . . .
of heaving torso and stretching limbs and beckoning
fingers and spiraling vertebrae, unwinding from
sincerity into sensuality, wistfulness into want.
A Dance of Need . . .
of desperately reaching arms that have nothing to
hold on to, straining neck, empty eyes, iron lungs,
Searching for light, suffocated in darkness.
A Dance of Confusion . . .
of snapping head, darting eyes, ragged breath,
lurching back—Where Am I Going? What Am I
Looking For?
A Dance of Power . . .
of slamming fists and pounding feet, fierce hips,
contracting ribcage. Raising a raging flame
from within, Set the World on Fire!
A Dance of Revelation . . .
of soaring wings and weightless legs and swooping
skirt and trip of ascension up from the mundane
toward the shining.
A Dance For You.

— *Rachel Rosner*

My Beloved Music

It is the one thing I can depend on
I can rest only when the soothing beat of a
    song is throbbing through my head

I can rely on music to share my sorrow
When I am so despairingly sad
I can lie on my bed sobbing my hot tears,
While the tones of unpretentious flutes float
    around me.

I can rely on my music to share my joy with
When I am ecstatic with happiness,
I grab a hairbrush,
And sing as loud as I can
With the wonderful sounds bursting out of that
    plain silver box
I can rely on it as something to let my anger out
When I run up to my room,
I yell down at my damned parents
The scream of electric guitars and the driving
    drumbeat annoys them.
It makes me feel so good

I can rely on it to keep me company,
When I am walking alone and the loneliness
    begins to set in,
I look about cautiously to see if anyone
    is around.
Then I burst out with the notes of a song,
The song is for me and only me.

The hard long hours of school
My body aches for the sound of
Lovely tones of flutes,
Screeching electric guitars,
Jazzy saxophones,
And some hero's voice
Booming out of the thing that is so dear to me,
My beloved radio.

— *Rachel Zindler*

To Write

Scrawling wonders of the world on an open
    sea of paper.
Opening magical gates of overwhelming
    language,
intricate description,
questions without answers,
and imagery beyond conception.

Leaving listeners and readers alike
in awe of my writing:
A noisy classroom turned quiet,
Aggravated parents turned proud.
A sullen special someone turned honored.

Steady rolling rhythms, ready-made rhymes
that fall into place easily
not straining the poem
or straying from the idea.

Line breaks and spaces,
letting the reader hear my voice.

A gift that lets me be heard,
lets me speak for others,
write what others think.

And I know, I could not ask
for a better gift.

— *David Modigliani*

Glossary of Terms*

Address	a poem that speaks to (addresses) a person or an object. Technically called "apostrophe."
Alliteration	repetition of initial sounds of words, usually consonants.
Animism	the belief that natural objects and phenomena possess souls or consciousness.
Apostrophe	an address to someone not present.
Assonance	repetition without rhyme of vowel sounds in stressed syllables. Assonance is sometimes used instead of direct rhyme.
Ballad	a simple narrative poem written in quatrains, often with the rhyme pattern ABCB, originally meant to be sung. Popular in fifteenth century England, it is a common form in Appalachia, in cowboy songs and poems, in folk and labor songs, and in some popular songs. English Romantic poets and contemporary poets have adapted this form to their literary ballads. Coleridge's "The Rime of the Ancient Mariner" is a well-known example.
Blank verse	poetic lines of approximately ten syllables, usually with five stresses (iambic pentameter), without rhymed end words. Marlowe, Shakespeare, and Milton ("Paradise Lost") were virtuosos of this form. Wordsworth, Browning, and Frost gradually used this form to get closer and closer to colloquial speech. See Frost's "Mending Wall."
Blues poems	a form borrowed from the blues, music based on work songs and "field hollers" of the Deep South, with roots in African music. Made popular in the 1900's, it has evolved into many current genres of music including rock and roll, jazz, rhythm and blues, and rap. The traditional blues stanza often has a first line, a second line which repeats the first with some slight variation, and a third line which rhymes with lines one and two. Langston Hughes was the first American poet to borrow either content, structure, or both from the blues for his own poems.
Chant	poems often spoken aloud in a rhythmic pattern, which may use repetition of phrases or parallel structure of words to accentuate the cadence. This form, which probably began with prehistoric peoples creating spells and incantations, is often associated with religious or spiritual ceremonies, sports events, and contemporary poems that wish to evoke the primitive insistent qualities of sound and language.
Cinquain	either a five-line stanza or a syllabic form comprised of five lines with two, four, six, eight, and two syllables, respectively.
Concrete image	an image that evokes a particular sense.
Concrete poem	a poem in which the arrangement of words or letters on the page is integral to the meaning.

* The *Handbook of Poetic Forms,* Ron Padgett, ed., and the *Poetry Handbook,* by Babette Deutsch, were referred to in preparing this Glossary of Terms.

Glossary of Terms *(continued)*

Consonance   a pair or group of words in which the final consonants of the stressed syllables agree but the vowels differ.

Couplet   a couple, or pair, of lines of poetry, usually rhymed. Heroic couplets are iambic pentameter couplets.

Figurative language   discourse in which the literal meaning of words is disregarded in order to show or imply a relationship between diverse things. Such language is made up of figures of speech (or tropes), which include simile, metaphor, and personification.

Free verse   while free of the strict rules of meter and rhyme, free verse allows the poet to strive for patterns close to his or her own thought and breath patterns, creating a personal rhythm. Walt Whitman saw free verse as the expression of democracy, and his writing, which left behind European influence, created a new movement in American poetry.

Haiku   a three-line poem from Japanese tradition, based on seventeen sounds. In America, we have interpreted this as three lines with syllables as follows: 5, 7, 5. It is a brief poem, usually about a common experience or a natural object, that records the essence of a moment, linking nature to human nature.

Iambic pentameter   a verse line of ten syllables creating five beats, or feet, each foot comprised of an unstressed syllable followed by a stressed one. It is the meter of heroic couplets, sonnets, and blank verse, used so brilliantly by Shakespeare, Marlowe, Milton, Wordsworth, and many others up to the present day.

Image   descriptive language that evokes a picture or resonates with one of the other four senses in the reader's mind.

Line break   the end of the poetic line as it creates a visual shape for the poem. The line break does not necessarily coincide with the end of the sentence or phrase.

Metaphor   language that implies a relationship between two things, in which similarity is a significant feature, thereby changing our apprehension of one or both.

Meter   the abstract pattern that results when rhythm is formally organized. It imposes on verse a regular recurrence of durations, stresses, or syllables that parcel a line into equal divisions of time called the foot.

Ode   an ancient form, a song (from the Greek word *aeidein*—to sing) invented by Pindar nearly 2,500 years ago in Greece that exalts and often addresses a person or a dignified theme. In more recent literature, poets have discarded many aspects of formality and structure but have kept the intensity and sense of exaltation. Pablo Neruda, in his *Odas Elementales (Odes to Simple Things)*, uses exalted, spontaneous language to celebrate ordinary objects: lemons, watermelons, fleas, socks, etc.

Parallel structure   a parallel arrangement of parts of speech in successive lines of verse ordered to build rhythm and momentum. It derives from tribal chant and oral tradition.

Persona   a poetic device by which the poet speaks through a voice other than his or her own. The voice might be that of another person—living or historic or invented—or an object, animal, even an abstract concept such as Anger or War.

Personification   to give human attributes to a thing or an idea.

Glossary of Terms *(continued)*

Praise poem	in order to praise the poem's subject, the poet may use some or all of these devices: a profusion of language, elevated diction, a piling up of sense images, an exuberance of feeling, hyperbole, parallel structure, stream of consciousness, and untraditional punctuation.
Prose poem	an intermediary form between poetry and prose, written without regard to line break. While it appears to look no different from a paragraph of prose, the poet's rhythms, condensed and figurative language, assonance and consonance, and other poetic techniques should distinguish the prose poem from narrative prose which has plot and character.
Quatrain	a stanza of four lines, rhymed or unrhymed.
Refrain	a reoccurring phrase, stanza, or chorus.
Rhyme	words whose final vowels and consonants are the same. There are many subtleties of rhyme involving slant rhyme or internal rhyme which also enhance the sound pleasures of the poem.
Sestina	a form that evolved during the Middle Ages in Europe, comprised of six unrhymed stanzas of six lines each in which the words at the ends of the first stanza's lines recur in a rolling pattern at the ends of all the other lines. The sestina then concludes with a tercet (three-line stanza) that also uses all six end words, two to a line.
Simile	a comparison between two images or ideas using "like" or "as."
Slant rhyme	nearly rhyming words that have similar vowels or similar consonants, but not both.
Sonnet	a lyric poem with fourteen lines written in iambic pentameter. Usually three quatrains and a couplet, or an octet and a sestet. Modern sonnets have experimented with variations on these rules.
Stanza	lines of verse grouped so as to compose a pattern that is usually repeated in the poem.
Syllabics	poems based on a certain number of syllables per line or verse.
Symbol	a word or an image that signifies something other than what it represents and that, even when denoting a physical, limited thing, carries enlarging connotations so that it has the reality, vivid yet ambiguous, the emotional power, and the suggestiveness of a compelling dream or an archetypal myth.
Tercet	a stanza comprised of three lines, usually rhymed. William Carlos Williams and Mary Oliver are two contemporary poets who use a three-line stanza (without rhyme) to capture natural American phrasing.
Tetrameter	a line of poetry with four beats or feet. William Blake's "The Tyger" is written in tetrameter.
Tone	the feature of a poem that shows the poet's attitude toward a theme, speaker, person addressed in the poem, or reader.
Villanelle	a cyclical form, used by the troubadours in Medieval France in the 1500's, comprised of five three-line stanzas followed by one four-line stanza. It is based on two rhymes and on two repeating lines: line one and line three of the first stanza, which alternate as last lines to succeeding stanzas. The final stanza uses both line one and line three as the final couplet.

A Way of Writing

A writer is not so much someone who has something to say as he is someone who has found a process that will bring about new things he would not have thought of if he had not started to say them. That is, he does not draw on a reservoir; instead, he engages in an activity that brings to him a whole succession of unforeseen stories, poems, essays, plays, laws, philosophies, religions, or—but wait!

Back in school from the first when I began to try to write things, I felt this richness. One thing would lead to another; the world would give and give. Now, after twenty years or so of trying, I live by that certain richness, an idea hard to pin, difficult to say, and perhaps offensive to some. For there are strange implications in it.

One implication is the importance of just plain receptivity. When I write, I like to have an interval before me when I am not likely to be interrupted. For me, this means usually the early morning, before others are awake. I get pen and paper, take a glance out of the window (often it is dark out there), and wait. It is like fishing. But I do not wait very long, for there is always a nibble—and this is where receptivity comes in. To get started I will accept anything that occurs to me. Something always occurs, of course, to any of us. We can't keep from thinking. Maybe I have to settle for an immediate impression: it's cold or hot, or dark, or bright, or in between! Or—well, the possibilities are endless. If

I put down something, that thing will help the next thing come, and I'm off. If I let the process go on, things will occur to me that were not at all in my mind when I started. These things, odd or trivial as they may be, are some-how connected. And if I let them string out, surprising things will happen.

If I let them string out . . . Along with initial receptivity, then there is another readiness: I must be willing to fail. If I am to keep on writing, I cannot bother to insist on high standards. I must get into action and not let anything stop me, or even slow me much. By "standards" I do not mean "correctness"—spelling, punctuation, and so on. These details become mechanical for anyone who writes for a while. I am thinking about such matters as social significance, positive values, consistency, etc. I resolutely disregard these. Something better, greater, is happening! I am following a process that leads so wildly and originally into new territory that no judgment can at the moment be made about values, significance, and so on. I am making something new, something that has not been judged before. Later others—and maybe I myself—will make judgments. Now, I am headlong to discover. Any distraction may harm the creating.

— *William Stafford*
from Writing the Australian Crawl

Bibliography and Suggested Readings

Anthologies

Adewale and Maja-Pearce, eds. *The Heinemann Book of African Poetry in English*. Portsmouth, NH: Heinemann,1990.

Adoff, Arnold, ed. *Celebrations, A New Anthology of Black American Poetry*. Chicago: Follett, 1977.

———. *I Am the Darker Brother*. New York: Collier/Macmillan, 1968.

———. *Poetry of Black America*. New York: Harper & Row, 1973.

Allison, Alexander, et. al., eds. *The Norton Anthology of Poetry*, 3rd ed. New York: W.W. Norton & Co., 1983.

Anglesey, Zoe, ed. *Ixok Amar Go: Central American Women's Poetry For Peace*. Penobscot, ME: Granite Press,1987.

Bradley, John, ed. *Atomic Ghost, Poets Respond to the Nuclear Age*. Minneapolis: Coffee House Press, 1995.

Barnstone, Aliki, and Willis Barnstone. *A Book of Women Poets from Antiquity to Now*. New York: Schocken Books, 1980.

Bankier, Joanna, et. al. *The Other Voice: Twentieth-Century Women's Poetry in Translation*. New York: W.W. Norton & Co.

Bierhorst, John, ed. *In the Trail of the Wind*. (Native American poems) New York: Dell, 1971.

Binder, Robert M., and Charles L. Squier, eds. *The Sonnet, An Anthology*. New York: Washington Square Press, 1987.

Bly, Robert. *News of the Universe*. New York: Sierra Club Books, 1980.

Bruchac, Joseph, ed. *Breaking Silence, An Anthology of Contemporary Asian American Poets*. Greenfield Center, NY: Greenfield Review Press, 1983.

———. *Songs from This Earth on Turtle's Back*. Greenfield Center, NY: Greenfield Review Press, 1983.

———. *The Next World: Poems by Third World Americans*. Trumansburg, NY: The Crossing Press, 1978.

Buchwalk, Emilie, and Ruth Roston, eds. *This Sporting Life*. Minneapolis, MN: Milkweed Editions, 1987.

Carlson, Lori M., ed. *Cool Salsa, Bilingual Poems on Growing Up Latino in the United States*. New York: Henry Holt and Co., 1994.

Cockburn, Victor, and Judith Steinbergh. *Where I Come From! Songs and Poems from Many Cultures*. (two cassette tapes and text in twelve languages with translations) Brookline, MA: Talking Stone Press, 1992.

Ellman, Richard, and Robert O'Clair. *The Norton Anthology of Modern Poetry*. New York: W.W. Norton & Co., 1973.

Empringham, Toni, ed. *Fiesta in Aztlan*. Santa Barbara, CA: *Chicano Poetry*. Capra Press, 1982.

Featherstone, Simon, ed. *War Poetry, An Introductory Reader.* New York: Routledge, 1995.

Feelings, Tom, ed. *Soul Looks Back in Wonder.* (anthology of African-American poets with drawings by Tom Feelings) New York: Dial Books, 1993.

Flores, Angel, et. al. *The Defiant Muse: Hispanic Feminist Poems from the Middle Ages to the Present.* New York: The Feminist Press at the City University, 1986.

Forché, Carolyn, ed. *Against Forgetting, Twentieth Century Poetry of Witness.* New York: W. W. Norton and Co., 1993.

Ford, R.A.D., trans. *Russian Poetry, A Personal Anthology.* Canada: Mosaic Press, 1984.

Foss, Phillip, ed. *The Clouds Threw This Light.* Santa Fe, NM: Institute of American Indian Arts Press, 1983.

Haba, James, ed. *Bill Moyers: The Language of Life—A Festival of Poets.* New York: Doubleday, 1995.

Harris, Marie, and Kathleen Aguero. *An Ear to the Ground.* Athens, GA: University of Georgia Press, 1989.

Harrison, Michael, and Christopher Stuart-Clark, eds. *Peace and War.* New York: Oxford University Press, 1989.

Hirschfelder, Arlene B. and Beverly R. Singer, eds. *Rising Voices: Writings of Young Native Americans.* New York: Scribner, 1992.

Honey, Maureen, ed. *Shadowed Dreams.* (women's Poetry of the Harlem Renaissance) New York: Rutgers Press, 1989.

Janeczko, Paul B. *Going Over to Your Place, Poems for Each Other.* Scarsdale, NY: Bradbury Press, 1987.

———. *The Music of What Happens Poems That Tell Stories.* New York: Orchard Books, 1988.

———. *This Delicious Day.* New York: Orchard Books, 1987.

———. *Pocket Poems.* Bradbury Scarsdale, NY: Press, 1985.

———. *Strings: A Gathering of Family Poems.* Scarsdale, NY: Bradbury Press, 1984.

———. *Poetspeak, In Their Work and About Their Work.* Scarsdale, NY: Bradbury Press, 1983.

Jordan, June, ed. *Soulscript, Afro-American Poetry.* (some by black teenagers, now poets) New York: Zenith/Doubleday, 1970.

Kherdian, David, ed. *I Sing the Song of Myself.* New York: Greenwillow Books, 1978.

Kramer, Aaron, ed. *On Freedom's Side, An Anthology of American Poems of Protest.* New York: Macmillan, 1972.

Knudson, R.R., and May Swenson. *American Sports Poems.* New York: Orchard Books, 1988.

Koch, Kenneth, and Kate Farrell. *Talking to the Sun.* New York: Metropolitan Museum of Art/Holt, Rinehart, 1985.

Larrick, Nancy, ed. *Bring Me All of Your Dreams.* New York: M. Evans & Co., 1980.

———. *Crazy to Be Alive in Such a Strange World.* New York: M. Evans & Co., 1977.

———. *Room for Me and a Mountain Lion.* New York: M. Evans & Co., 1974.

———. *On City Streets: An Anthology of Poetry.* New York: M. Evans & Co., 1968.

Lewis, Richard. *Out of the Earth I Sing: Poetry and Songs of Primitive Peoples of the World.* New York: W. W. Norton & Co., 1968.

———. *Still Waters of the Air, Poems by Three Modern Spanish Poets.* New York: Dial Press, 1970.

Lifton, Robert Jay, and Nicholas Humphrey, eds. *In a Dark Time,* Cambridge, MA: Harvard University Press, 1984.

Lim, Shirley, Geok-lin, and Mayumi Tsutakawa. *The Forbidden Stitch, An Asian American Women's Anthology.* Corvalis, OR: Calyx Books, 1989.

Lorie, Dick, and Mark Pawlak. *Smart like Me, High School Age Writing.* Brooklyn: Hanging Loose Press, 1989.

Lowenfels, Walter. *The Writing on the Wall.* New York: Doubleday, 1969.

Lueders, Edward, and Primus St. John. *Zero Makes Me Happy.* Scott, Glenview, IL: Foresman & Co., 1976.

Mazer, Norma Fox, and Marjorie Lewis, eds. *Waltzing on Water, Poetry by Women.* New York: Dell, 1989.

McDonald, Ian, and Stewart Brown, eds. *The Heinemann Book of Caribbean Poetry.* London: Heinemann Books, 1992.

Miller, E. Ethelbert, ed. *In Search Of Color Everywhere—A Collection of African-American Poetry.* New York: Stewart, Tabori & Chang, 1994.

Morrison, Lillian, ed. *Rhythm Road, Poems to Move To.* New York: Lothrop Lee, 1988.

Niatum, Duane, ed. *Harper's Anthology of Twentieth Century Native American Poetry.* New York: Harper and Row, 1988.

Oresick, Peter, and Nicholas Coles. *Working Classics: Poems on Industrial Life.* Urbana, IL: University of Illinois Press, 1990.

Phillips, J.J., et. al., eds. *The Before Columbus Foundation Poetry Anthology: Selections from the American Book Awards: 1980–1990.* New York: W. W. Norton & Co., 1992.

Reed, John, and Clive Wake. *A New Book of African Verse.* London: Heinemann Ltd., 1984.

Ritchie, Elisavietta, ed. *The Dolphin's Arc.* (ecology-related poems) College Park, MD: SCOP Publications, 1989.

Rosen, Kenneth, ed. *Voices of the Rainbow: Contemporary Poetry by Native Americans.* New York: Arcade Publishing, 1992.

Rothenberg, Jerome, ed. *Shaking the Pumpkin.* (Native-American poetry) New York: Doubleday, 1992.

———. *Technicians of the Sacred. A Range of Poetries from Africa, America, Asia, Europe, and Oceania.* Berkeley, CA: University of California Press, 1985.

Salkey, Andrew, ed. *Breaklight, the Poetry of the Caribbean.* New York: Doubleday, 1972.

Schiff, Hilda. *Holocaust Poetry.* New York: St. Martins Press, 1995.

Shihab Nye, Naomi. *This Same Sky, A Collection of Poems from Around the World, in English Translation.* New York: Four Winds Press, 1992.

Stetson, Erlene, ed. *Black Sister: Poetry By Black American Women, 1746–1980.* Bloomington, IN: Indiana University Press,1981.

Strickland, Dorothy, ed. *Listen Children: An Anthology of Black Literature.* New York: Bantam,1982.

Sullivan, Charles, ed. *Here Is My Kingdom: Hispanic-American Literature and Art for Young People.* New York: Harry N. Abrams, Inc.,1994.

———. *Children of Promise: African-American Literature & Art for Young People.* New York: Harry N. Abrams, Inc.,1991.

———. *America in Poetry*. New York: Abradale Press, Harry N. Abrams, Inc., 1988.

Thompson, Eileen. *Experiencing Poetry*. New York: Globe Books, l987. (poems, questions, and writing suggestions for grades 6–10)

Untermeyer, Louis. *Modern American Poetry/Modern British Poetry*. New York: Harcourt Brace,1958.

Volavkov'a Hana, ed. *I Never Saw Another Butterfly: Children's Drawings & Poems from Terezin Concentration Camp, 1942–1944*. New York: Schocken Books, 1993.

Individual Volumes

This is a sampling of books by authors from diverse cultures, some well known, others emerging and less easily found in common anthologies.

Agosín, Marjorie. *Circles of Madness: Mothers of the Plaza de Mayo (Circulos de locura: Madres de la Plaza de Mayo)*. Fredonia, NY: White Pine Press, 1992.

———. *Dear Ann Frank*. Washington, DC: Azol Editions, 1994.

Alegría, Claribel. *Fugues*. Willimantic, CT: Curbstone Press, 1993.

Alexie, Sherman. *The Business of FancyDancing*. Brooklyn, NY: Hanging Loose Press, 1992.

Allen, Paula Gunn. *Skins and Bones*. Albuquerque, NM: West End Press, 1988.

Angell, Barbara. *Games and Puzzles*. Cleveland: Cleveland State University Press, 1978.

Angelou, Maya. *Poems*. (selected from four books) New York: Bantam Books, 1986.

Baca, Jimmy Santiago. *Black Mesa Poems*. New York: New Directions, 1989.

Berrigan, Daniel. *Prison Poems*. New York: Viking, 1973.

Brathwaite, Edward Kamau. *X/Self*. (Caribbean poetry) New York: Oxford University Press, 1987.

Bloch, Chana, et. al., eds. *Selected Poetry of Yehuda Amichai*. New York: Harper & Row, 1986.

Brooks, Gwendolyn. *Selected Poems*. New York: Harper & Row, 1963.

———. *Blacks*. Chicago: The David Company, 1988.

Browning, Elizabeth Barrett. *Sonnets from the Portuguese and Other Love Poems*. New York: Doubleday, 1990.

Brutus, Dennis. *A Simple Lust*. (poems of exile from a South African jail) London: Heinemann, 1973.

Bursk, Christopher. *Places of Comfort, Places of Justice*. San Jose, CA: Humanities and Arts Press, 1987.

Cisneros, Sandra. *Loose Woman*. New York: Knopf, distributed by Random House, 1994.

Chin, Marily. *Dwarf Bamboo*. Greenfield Center, NY: Greenfield Review Press, 1987.

Ch'ing-Chao, Li. *Plum Blossoms*. Chapel Hill, NC: Carolina Wren Press, 1984.

Clifton, Lucille. *Next*. Brockport, NY: Boa Editions, Ltd., 1987.

Coles, Robert. *A Festering Sweetness, Poems of American People*. Pittsburgh: University of Pittsburgh Press, 1978.

Cummings, E.E. *100 selected poems*. New York: Grove Press, 1954.

Dao, Bei. *The August Sleepwalker*. New York: New Directions, 1988.

Dickinson, Emily. *I'm Nobody, Who Are You?* Barbara Holdridge, ed. Owings Mills, MD: Stemmer House, 1978.

Dove, Rita. *Museum.* Pittsburgh: Carnegie-Mellon, 1983.

Esbensen, Barbara Juster. *Cold Stars and Fireflies, Poems of the Four Seasons.* New York: Crowell, 1984.

Espada, Martín. *City of Coughing and Dead Radiators.* New York: W.W. Norton, 1993.

Fox, Siv Cedering. *The Blue Horse and Other Night Poems.* New York: Seabury Press, 1979.

Frost, Robert. *A Swinger of Birches.* (poems selected by Barbara Holdridge) Owings Mills, MD: Stemmer House, 1982.

———. *The Poetry of Robert Frost.* (edited by Edward Connery Lathem) New York: Holt, Rinehart & Winston, 1969.

Giovanni, Nikki. *Spin a Soft Black Song.* (urban and family poems) New York: Hill & Wang, 1971.

———. *My House.* New York: Morrow, 1972.

Harjo, Joy. *She Had Some Horses.* New York: Thunder's Mouth Press, 1983.

Hogan, Linda. *Savings.* Minneapolis, MN: Coffee House Press, 1988.

———. *Seeing Through the Sun.* Amherst, MA: University of Massachusetts Press, 1985.

Hughes, Langston. *Selected Poems.* New York: Vintage Classics, Random House, 1990.

Hughes, Ted. *Season Song.* New York: Viking, 1975.

———. *Under the North Star.* (animal poems) New York: Viking, 1981.

Hyett, Barbara. *In Evidence.* Pittsburgh: University of Pittsburgh Press, 1986.

Jordan, June. *Naming Our Destiny, New and Selected Poems.* New York: Thunder's Mouth Press, 1989.

Kendrick, Dolores. *The Women of Plums.* (voices of slave women) Andover, MA: Phillips Exeter Academy Press, 1989.

Kenny, Maurice. *Takonwatonti/Molly Brant: Poems of War.* Fredonia, NY: White Pine Press, 1992.

Kinnell, Galway. *Three Books.* Boston: Houghton Mifflin Co., 1993.

Komunyakaa, Yusef. *Neon Vernacular.* Hanover, NH: University/New England Press, 1993.

———. *Dien Cai Day.* Middletown, CT: Wesleyan University Press, 1988.

Knight, Etheridge. *The Essential Etheridge Knight.* Pittsburgh: University of Pittsburgh Press, 1986.

Kumin, Maxine. *The Long Approach.* New York: Viking, 1985.

Lawrence, D.H. *Birds, Beasts and the Third Thing.* New York: Viking, 1964.

Lee, Li-Young. *Rose.* Brockport, NY: BOA Ltd., 1986.

Levi, Primo. *Collected Poems.* Boston: Faber & Faber, 1988.

McKim, Elizabeth. *Boat of the Dream.* Brookline, MA: Talking Stone Press, 1989.

Merriam, Eve. *If Only I Could Tell You.* New York: Alfred A. Knopf, 1983.

Momaday, N. Scott. *In the Presence of the Sun.* New York: St. Martin's Press, 1992.

Neruda Pablo. *Five Decades: Poems 1925–1970.* New York: Grove Press, 1974.

Olds, Sharon. *The Dead and the Living.* New York: Alfred A. Knopf, 1983.

Oliver, Mary. *Dream Work.* Boston: Atlantic Monthly Press, 1986.

———. *American Primitive.* Boston: Little Brown, 1978.

———. *New and Selected Poems.* Boston: Beacon Press, 1992.

Ortiz Cofer, Judith. *Silent Dancing, A Partial Remembrance of a Puerto Rican Childhood,* 2nd ed. Houston: Arte Publico Press, 1991.

Piercy, Marge. *Circles on the Water, Selected Poems.* New York: Alfred A. Knopf, 1982.

Poe, Edgar Allan. *Complete Tales and Poems.* New York: Vintage Books, 1975.

Rushin, Kate. *The Black Back-Ups.* Ithaca, NY: Firebrand Press, 1993.

Sandburg, Carl. *Rainbows Are Made.* (selected by Lee Bennett Hopkins) New York: Harcourt Brace, 1982.

Savageau, Cheryl. *Home Country.* Cambridge, MA: Alice James Books, 1992.

Silko, Leslie Marmon. *Ceremony.* New York: Penguin Books, 1977.

Smith, Patricia. *Big Towns, Big Talk.* Cambridge, MA: Zoland Books, 1992.

Soto, Gary. *A Fire in My Hands.* New York: Scholastic Hardcover, 1977.

———. *Neighborhood Odes.* San Diego: Harcourt Brace, 1992.

Spivack. *The Beds We Lie In, Selected & New Poems.* Metuch, NJ: Scarecrow Press, 1986.

Steinbergh, Judith. *A Living Anytime.* Brookline, MA : Talking Stone Press, 1988.

———, and Victor Cockburn. *Feel Yourself in Motion,* Brookline, MA: Talking Stone Press, 1983.

Swenson, May. *New and Selected Things Taking Place.* Boston: Little, Brown & Co., 1978.

Tapahonso, Luci. *A Breeze Swept Through.* Albuquerque, NM: West End Press, 1987.

al Udhari, Abdullah, trans. *Victims of a Map, A Bilingual Anthology of Arabic Poetry.* (poets: Mahmud Darwish, Samih Al-Qasim, Adonis) London: Al Saqi Books, 1984.

Villanueva, Tino. *Shaking Off the Dark.* Houston: Arte Público Press, 1984.

Whitman, Ruth. *Tamsen Donner: A Woman's Journey.* Cambridge, MA: AliceJamesBooks, 1977.

———. *The Testing of Hanna Senesh.* Detroit: Wayne State University Press, 1986.

———. *Laughing Gas, New and Selected Poems.* Detroit: Wayne State University Press, 1990.

Whitman, Walt. *Poems.* (selected by Lee Bennett Hopkins) New York: Harcourt Brace, 1988.

Worth, Valerie. *All the Small Poems.* New York: Sunburst Book, Farrar, Straus, & Giroux, 1987.

Yan, Ke. *Poems on a Boy's Paintings.* Beijing, China: Foreign Language Press, 1981.

For Teachers

Brown, Bill, and Malcolm Glass. *Important Words, A Book for Poets and Writers.* Portsmouth, NH: Heinemann, 1991.

Cockburn, Victor. "The Uses of Folk Music and Songwriting in the Classroom." Arts as Education, *Harvard Educational Review,* Reprint Series #24. Cambridge, MA: 1992.

Dillard, Annie. *The Writing Life.* New York: Harper & Row, 1989.

Di Yanni, Robert. *Reading Poetry, An Anthology of Poems.* (teacher's guide included) New York: Random House School Division, 1989.

Goldberg, Natalie. *Wild Mind, Living the Writer's Life.* New York: Bantam, 1990.

———. *Writing Down the Bones, Freeing the Writer Within.* Boston: Shambhala, 1986.

Grossman, Florence. *Listening to the Bells, Learning to Read Poetry by Writing Poetry.* Portsmouth, NH: Heinemann, 1991.

Hoffman, Eva. *Lost in Translation, a Life in a New Language.* New York: E.P. Dutton, 1989.

Hull, Gloria T. *Color, Sex, and Poetry.* (on three women writers of the Harlem Renaissance) Bloomington: Indiana University Press, 1987.

Johnson, David M. *Word Weaving, A Creative Approach to Teaching and Writing Poetry.* Urbana, IL: NCTE, 1990.

Kennedy, X.J. *An Introduction to Poetry,* 6th ed. New York: Scott, Foresman & Co., 1986.

Levertov, Denise. *The Poet in the World.* New York: New Directions, 1960.

Livingston, Myra Cohn. *The Child as Poet, Myth or Reality.* Boston: Horn Book, 1984.

McKim, Elizabeth, and Judith Steinbergh. *Beyond Words, Writing Poems with Children.* Brookline, MA: Talking Stone Press, 1992.

Nims, John Frederick. *Western Wind.* (high school and college level text) New York: Random House, 1974.

Padgett, Ron, ed. *Handbook of Poetic Forms.* New York: Teachers & Writers Collaborative, 1987.

Rilke, Rainer Maria. *Letters to a Young Poet.* New York: W.W. Norton & Co., 1934.

Scully, James. *Modern Poetics.* (poets' essays on poetry) New York: McGraw-Hill, 1965.

Simonson, Rick, et. al. *Multi-Cultural Literacy.* Saint Paul: Graywolf Press, 1988.

Slapin, Beverly, and Doris Seales. *Through Indian Eyes.* Philadelphia: New Society Publishers, 1992.

Stafford, William. *Writing the Australian Crawl, Views on the Writer's Vocation.* Ann Arbor, MI: University of Michigan Press, 1978.

Steinbergh, Judith. "Chandra," *Children's Voices: Children Talk About Literacy.* Portsmouth, NH: Heinemann, 1993.

———. "To Arrive in Another World: Poetry Language Development, and Culture," Arts as Education, *Harvard Educational Review,* Reprint Series #24. Cambridge, MA: 1992.

———. *Reading and Writing Poetry.* (grades K–4) New York: Scholastic Books, 1994.

Tsujimoto, Joseph I. *Teaching Poetry Writing to Adolescents.* Urbana, IL: NCTE.

Vendler, Helen, ed. *Voices and Visions: The Poet in America.* New York: Random House.

Walker, Margaret. *How I Wrote Jubilee, and Other Essays on Life and Literature.* New York: The Feminist Press at NYU, 1990.

Whitman, Ruth. *Becoming a Poet.* Boston: Source-Process-Practice, Writer, Inc., 1982.

Miscellaneous Resources

Audiocassettes

Catalogue of Poetry on Tape. (poets reading their own work*)* Poets' Audio Center, Watershed, Caedmon, New Letters, Spoken Arts, and other publishers. P.O. Box 50145 Willow, Washington, DC 20091; 1-800-366-9105 or 1-202-722-9106.

The Poet's Voice. (readings and commentary by poets including Robert Frost, Pablo Neruda, Dylan Thomas) Unterberg Poetry Center. WNYC radio, "Arts and Ideas," New York; 617-876-WGBH.

Videocassettes

The Language of Life. (Bill Moyers interviews and readings with poets including Claribel Alegría, Jimmy Santiago Baca, Robert Bly, Marilyn Chin, Carolyn Forche, Naomi Shihab Nye, Daisy Zamora) PBS Video.

Lannon Literary Videos. (60–90 minute videotaped readings and interviews with 47 poets and prose writers) Lannon Foundation, 5401 McConnell Ave., Los Angeles, CA 90066; 310-306-1004. Distributed by Small Press Distributor, Berkeley, CA, 1-800-869-7553, or by American Poetry Archives at San Francisco State University, 415-338-1056.

The Power of the Word. (Bill Moyers interviews and poetry readings: "The Power of the Word," "Ancestral Voices," "Dancing on the Edge of the Road," "The Living Language," "The Simple Acts of Life," "Voices of Memory") PBS Video, 1989.

Voices and Visions. (PBS television series and college credit course, 13 one-hour programs on modern American poetry) Annenberg/CPB Project, 1111 16th St., N.W., Washington, DC 20036; (202) 955-5251.

CD-ROM

Poetry in Motion. Ron Mann, ed. (18 modern poets perform and discuss their work) Voyager Co., 1 Bridge St., Irvington, NY 10553; 1-800-446-2001.

Poetry Magazines and Small Presses

International Directory of Little Magazines and Small Presses. (cross-indexed annual directory) Dustbooks, P.O. Box 100, Paradise, CA 95967.

Periodicals that publish youth poetry

Claremont Review (ages 13–19)
4890 Wesley Rd.
Victoria, B.C. V8Y 1Y9
Canada

Cricket (ages 9–13)
Box 300
Peru, IL 61354

Hanging Loose

Merlyn's Pen: The National Magazine of Student Writing, Senior Edition
Merlyn's Pen, Inc.
Box 1058
E. Greenwich, RI 02818-0964

Poetry Northwest
University of Washington
4045 Brooklyn Ave.
Seattle, WA 98105

Poetry: USA Quarterly
U.S.A. Publishers
2569 Maxwell Ave.
Oakland, CA 94601

This and That (English and Russian)
Gnosis Press
Box 42
Prince St.
New York, NY 10012

Yale Series of Younger Poets
Yale University Press
Box 209040
New Haven, CT 06520

About the Authors

Fredric Lown has been teaching English, social studies, and drama in the greater Boston public schools for the past twenty-three years. He is currently teaching English at the Runkle School in Brookline, Massachusetts.

In the capacity of his teaching jobs, Lown has traveled with groups of his students to Washington, DC, and Mount Cardigan, New Hampshire, on many occasions. As a drama teacher, he has directed five eighth-grade plays including "West Side Story" and "HMS Pinafore."

Lown is an active advocate for children. He codirected the Brookline School Staff Child Care Center in the early 1980's, and he served on the Board of Directors for the Edna Stein Academy, a school for troubled children, in the early 1990's.

During the 1994–1995 academic year, Lown was awarded an A.C.L.S. humanities fellowship to study poetry at Harvard University.

He is married to Dr. Beth Lown, an internist, and is the father of three children ages seven, fourteen, and sixteen.

Judith W. Steinbergh has been teaching poetry in the schools since 1971. She was Poet-in-Residence in the Hamilton-Wenham, Massachusetts, public schools from 1977–1981 and in the Brookline public schools since 1981, as well as leading workshops for grades K–12 in over sixty urban, suburban, and rural schools. She has trained teachers and been adjunct faculty at Wheelock and Lesley colleges and at Tufts University. She has published four books of poetry (the most recent is *A Living Anytime*, Talking Stone Press), two texts: *Reading and Writing Poetry, A Guide for Teachers K–4* (Scholastic) and co-authored with Elizabeth McKim, *Beyond Words, Writing Poems with Children*. With Victor Cockburn of Troubadour, Inc., she created seven tapes and two CDs of songs and poetry for children, including the award-winning *Where I Come From! Songs and Poems from Many Cultures* and *Get Ready for Boston! Exploring Boston and Its Neighborhoods in Songs, Poems, and Stories.*

Index

Credits